THE BOOK
OF JOB

THE BOOK
OF JOB

God's Faithfulness in Troubled Times

DR. JIM HALLA

AMBASSADOR INTERNATIONAL
GREENVILLE, SOUTH CAROLINA & BELFAST, NORTHERN IRELAND

www.ambassador-international.com

THE BOOK OF JOB

God's Sovereignty and Job's Suffering, Suspicion, and Success

ISBN: 978-1-62020-731-4

eISBN: 978-1-62020-750-5

Cover Design by Hannah Linder Designs
Interior Typesetting by Dentelle Design

AMBASSADOR INTERNATIONAL
411 University Ridge Suite B14
Greenville, SC 29609, USA
www.ambassador-international.com

AMBASSADOR BOOKS
The Mount
2 Woodstock Link
Belfast, BT6 8DD, Northern Ireland, UK
www.ambassador-international.com

The colophon is a trademark of Ambassador

Contents

Preface

JOB, THE BOOK AND THE man, is well-known even in the public arena. However, the main character of the book is the Triune God. Some have suggested that the book of Job focuses on the larger problem of evil in a good God's world. From that perspective, various attempts have been made to defend God's goodness and power in view of the existence of evil. *Theodicy* refers to the justification of God, His Being, goodness, and omnipotence in view of the existence of evil and the presence of hard times and suffering. However, I believe that vision limits the Holy Spirit and the believer's use of the book.

In my view, the book's major focus is on the very essence of God and the believer's relationship to Him in all types of God's providence. Others tend to agree and view the book as cataloguing the development of Job to become not only the most righteous among mortals, but the most wise (*An Old Testament Theology: An Exegetical, Canonical, and Thematic Approach*: Bruce Waltke, Zondervan, 2007; pages 927-945). Therefore, the book has a relational emphasis highlighting who God is in relation to His people and His world. The relationships, which include those between God, Satan, and heavenly beings; those between God, Job, and the friends; and those between Job and his friends.

Further, the book specifically focuses on covenant relationships with the possibility of failed promises and un-trustworthiness on God's part as perceived by Job. Predominately, the book focuses on God's character as the one and only trustworthy and caring Promisemaker, Promisekeeper, Master, and Controller.

Job's experience and response is based on his changing view of God and himself. He is pictured as a student in a major theology class, a preserver, a doubter, a demander, and a lawyer. The book, rightly understood, helps believers interpret and respond to life situations which are actually God's providence in a God-honoring way. Job learned God's way which was a blessing to him, his family, and his friends. Moreover, it honored God and helped prepare believers in all ages for the cross. Job began to correctly interpret God and the circumstances through the grid of a personal relationship with God and God with him. He latched on to God's word as his interpretive grid rather than his circumstances (hard or easy), his experience, his reasoning divorced completely or partially from biblical truth and or his feelings.

Introduction

ALMOST EVERYONE KNOWS THE STORY of Job. The book of Job has been extensively evaluated and many authors have contributed various opinions. However, the author, the date, where he lived, and the site from which he wrote are unknown. The author may have been a prophet and frequently used the Israelite covenant name *Yahweh*. Most theologians consider the author a literary genius. He puts the speeches from the mouth of Job and the four friends in such a way that drama builds to a climax. The climax in one sense is unexpected as Job enters into the very presence of the great I AM but not as one in charge. The author gives Christians in every age a peek into the heavenlies and the workings of God's good and powerful control in the midst of Job's troubles and his lawyer-approach to God and them. It is a book for all believers in all seasons no matter their spiritual maturity.

The book of Job probably predates the book of Genesis and may have been edited by someone such as Moses. Many scholars believe that the book of Job is one of the oldest books in the world. The best assumption is that it was written between the time of Moses and Ezra. Based on the spelling of the words, the book was probably written in the seventh century B.C.

The book contains no reference to features that were prominent in Israel's history: the monarchy, the temple, the prophets, or any of Israel's major historical events such as the Exodus. Job probably lived during the patriarchal period and functioned as a tribal chieftain or as an elder in a major town (29:7). The fact that he offered sacrifices places him before the Law of Moses which designated that only the Aaronic priesthood could perform sacrifices.

The book is one long narrative in poetic form (chapters 3 to chapter 42, verse 6). Job was a monotheist (23:13) as were his friends. The name *Yahweh*, God's covenant name, is used some twenty-seven times in the book, all in chapters 1-2, 38-42 except once in chapter 12 (12:9) indicating that the author was an Israelite. The book contains the longest continuous speech by God recorded in the Bible (four chapters — chapters 38-41); it also contains the longest recorded speeches of Satan (two interactions between God and Satan in two chapters — chapters 1-2).

Job lived in the unidentified land of Uz, which was a territory outside of Israel east of the Jordan. The author presents Job as a "good man," a man of integrity, fearing God and shunning evil, and the greatest of all men of the east (1:1, 3; 2:3). God blessed Job with material prosperity (1:3). He was in covenant with God because God was in covenant with him (1:1-5). In that sense, he was like Christ. Don't miss that point. I refer to it throughout the book.

Job was blameless and upright, caring for and interceding for his wife and children and helping others (1:5; 4:3-4). However, he had problems — trouble — from the hand of God. Many speak of the suffering of Job. We need to be careful here. Too often the term *suffering* is undefined and is focused on the subjective — the person's feelings which too often control his or her response. I prefer the generic term *trouble*. Labels have significance. Trouble must be understood as an expression of God's providence: God's control of His world, His way for His glory, and for the good of His people (Genesis 50:15-21; Romans 8:28-29). "Things" providentially happened to Job, and Job responded based on his theology. Everyone is a theologian because everyone has a belief about God and is in a proper or improper relation with Him.

God took Job to school as He does all of His people. Job was in school initially as an honor student (1:20-22; 2:10) and later as we shall see, as one who took God to court. Eventually, he graduated *magna sum laude* but only after he entered into God's presence (40:1-5; 42:2-6). However, while Job was in class there was concern as to his final grade. Would Job curse God thereby demonstrating to the world that Satan was right, and that God and His people were losers? Or was God who He claimed to be? If He was, what value did that knowledge have for Job? How would it lead to Job's victory and God's victory?

We must remember that God's providence which some people term *life* includes every situation and person that is present or has been present in someone's life. *Life* never just "is." *Life* has no life of its own! *Life* has an Originator and Sustainer (Acts 17:24). In Job's case, his hard times were not simply *life* and they were not of his own doing. This added to Job's dilemma — how can bad things happen to someone who has a personal and vital relationship with God? That question forces every person to the cross in an effort to plumb the depths of God's ways (1 Corinthians 1:18-31, Isaiah 55:8-9). Based on his circumstances, Job wondered why his relationship with God meant so little. He thought that a vital relationship with God should protect and even immunize him from hard times.

What happened to him was beyond his understanding. Early on Job could not and did not understand the cross. This fact is an important one. Later I consider four passages that refer to a mediator, arbiter, or a "go-between." When Job graduated, he understood so much more. Moreover, God had him act as a type of Christ when he offered sacrifices for his three friends (Job 42). Job had come "a long way."

According to Rabbi Kushner who had a child with progeria, God is either not good but powerful or powerful and not good (*When Bad Things Happen to Good People*, New York: Avon Books, 1988; pages 42-43). He made conclusions about God and people, himself included, based on his circumstances, understanding, and feelings. Many people assume and demand the right to know where God is "in all of this" and what He is "up to." Further, many believe that they have a right to judge what kind of Being God is based on "life" and circumstances that occur in the world. Others may acknowledge God but only as they know Him. Begrudgingly, they acknowledge the fact that there is no escaping God — He is man's environment (Psalm 139). However, they have set themselves on the horns of a dilemma: is God's presence a blessing or a burden? For Job, initially God's presence was manifested by silence and assumed un-involvement. Job considered God and His providence — control — a burden (3:13, 17, 26; 13:3, 6; 16:21; 23:2; 31:35; 33:7-11, 35-37; 40:2).

Job is mentioned only once in the New Testament (James 5:11). In that passage, James highlights Job's perseverance. It is interesting that Job was not included in the believer's "hall of faith" (Hebrews 11).

Many have highlighted major themes in the book including the reality of God's sovereignty as Controller and Creator; *suffering* and trials, so-called God's hard providences; Satan as a created being and God's use of him as His agent; the Creator-creature distinction; and one-on-one ministry as evidenced by four counselors. As I have alluded to previously, there are several other key issues in the book of Job that deserve our attention. These include the issue of relationships — God to

individuals, individuals to God, and individuals to others —
and their theological significance; the beauty of an intimate
knowledge of God and self; a robust understanding of the
subject of problems/hard times; a proper understanding
of humiliation and humility; a proper response to God's
providence in its various forms which is a response to God;
and most importantly, a proper a redemptive focus that leads
to a proper understanding of the cross which leads to victory
in every problem. God chose the context of tough times as His
classroom to teach Job and all believers throughout the ages.
Such is one lesson of the cross (1 Corinthians 1:18-31).

I propose to look at the book under four headings:

- **Sovereignty**: I am speaking of God's control, power,
  and authority and man's view of it and response to it
  especially when faced with unpleasantness.

- **Suffering**: I am speaking of God's providence, man's
  response to God, and man's response in the midst of the
  situation. The term *suffering* so often influences people
  to focus on the subjective. In the original language of
  the New Testament a term commonly used for suffering
  literally means experience (*pascho* and *pathema*). In that
  sense it is a colorless term. Another common term for
  trouble and affliction is *thlipsis*, Other terms are used
  that are translated as pain and grief, (including *lupeo*
  and its derivatives). There are other words that attempt

to depict inner-man angst and vexation such as *tarasso*. The term suffering is most often used to refer to distress and hardship. It can refer to the situation itself or to the person's response to and in it. I believe that using the term to refer to God's providence helps us focus on God's truths and a proper response to God in the situation. That fact is what motivated Jesus. Jesus and Job were not victims of God and His ways. They were not victims to Satan. Job personally had witnessed God's power, control, goodness, and grace. God's providence changed and so did Job. The latter features, God's goodness and grace, were not emphasized by Job or his friends. Only as God directly revealed Himself did Job understand and value who God was and His ways. Only then did Job acknowledge his relationship with God and God's with him as a blessing and a privilege. Only then was he satisfied; prior to that he had lived the lie.

- **Suspicion**: especially on Job's part. Job's suspicion centered on the fact that he knew that he had a vital, healthy relationship with God. But to his way of thinking, his circumstances indicated differently. Eventually, in response to God's providence (his losses, his physical problems, and the counsel of his wife and the friends), Job's cry was: "God, You owe me an explanation." He was suspicious of God and later, the three friends. Job was burdened with them and by their counsel. They were suspicious of Job. Moreover, the three friends thought they had God all figured-out. They counseled according to their view of God and His providence. They believed bad things happen to sinful people. They presented God primarily as a God of retribution. According to them, God's main function was to uphold this law and reward the righteous and punish the evil doer (*New Dictionary of Biblical Theology*; Desmond, Rosner, Carson, Goldsworthy; Inter-varsity Press, 206; pages 200-203). Moreover, they claimed this concept was not their own invention (Job 4:8; 8:8-13; 15:17-20). The law of retribution was a commonly held belief that was taught in the Old and New Testaments (Psalms 17:3; 18:20-28; 26:1-12; 44:17-22; Luke 13:1-5; John 9:1-3). It was agreed to by Job and a number of people as a way of vindication (Job 6:24; 13:23; 27:6, 31; 1 Samuel 12:3; 2 Kings 20:3). However, this truth is only part of God's story. The cross proves this fact! God rebuked the three friends for misrepresenting Him (Job 42:7). God's answer for Job, so they thought and counseled, was repentance. Moreover, God's call was only for Job and it did not concern them because they did not have hard times. They attempted to tie God's control and power into a neat package. There was a problem: their theology was flawed, truncated, and burdensome. Moreover, the cross and the Suffering Servant had no place in their theology and counsel.

- **Success**: success must be spelled God's way. God must be and will be glorified. Only then will the believer be blessed. In the end, relief will come to the believer as it did to Job. However, relief and victory will come God's way according to His timetable and in His way. Job discovered that God was not on Job's timetable. A corollary truth: God's people receive maximal benefit when God is glorified. This became apparent to all parties including Satan even though after chapter two Satan is not mentioned again in the book.

I repeat, the book of Job is more about God than Job. In a sense, God's *Godness* was at stake. Such it is with the cross. Therefore, the book points to Christ. Both Christ and Job, as did Joseph in the book of Genesis, moved from a position of exaltation to one of humiliation. Jesus placed Himself in that position and Job and Joseph were placed in their state of humiliation. As we shall see, unlike Jesus and Joseph, initially, Job failed to humble himself. Humiliation and humbling oneself are not synonymous. In the end, Job embraced God's plan of going down in order to come up by humbling himself. Such is the way of the cross. The book also focuses on relationships in the context of Job's problems and his response. In that sense, the book is for "everyman" in daily life. The book places God's control under the microscope of human reasoning devoid of biblical truth in varying degrees on the part of all involved. It brings biblical truth to the fore in order to settle the answer God's way. God purposefully governs His world for His glory and the good of the kingdom and each individual believer. The book of Job is a preview of the power of the cross rightly understood and Christ's life leading up to the cross. Job was a type of Christ as we shall see but he was not Him.

Application

1. Write out your view of God including who He is; what He has done; what He is doing, and what has promised to do, and how He does it. How do those truths influence you in daily life?

2. God is or God is not; God is good or He is bad; God is in control or He is not: how do you decide, when do you decide, and what are the results of those decisions?

3. Job faced his situations based on his view of God and himself: write out what God said about Job.

CHAPTER 1

In the Heavenlies

Job 1 and 2

THE BOOK OPENS WITH A statement about Job by God (1:1) which is repeated in Job 1:8 and Job 2:3. God is placed center stage as He gave His view of Job: *This man was blameless and upright; he feared God and shunned evil.* By this description God declared Job a wise God-fearer and a type of Christ (Proverbs 1:7; 9:10; 31:30; Psalm 1:1-3; 111:10; Job 28:28; Ecclesiastes 12:13-14). God's declaration regarding Job sets the stage for a cosmic showdown between God and Satan for the world to witness.

Chapters 1-2 present an audience between God and various beings in and of the unseen world. Satan's presence poses several problems and raises several issues. What is Satan doing in God's presence? What is the author teaching us about God and His relationship to creatures including Satan? What does the author mean when he speaks of sons of men or angels (Job 1:6 and 2:1: *One day the angels came to present themselves before the Lord and Satan also with them*; see 38:7)? In answering these questions we ask, as others have, who or what are sons of men or angels? The fact that the author described the circumstances the way he did is a vitally important point. It sets the stage for a proper understanding of the lessons taught by the Holy Spirit in the book of Job.

The meeting is a hearty acknowledgement that the beings were created, angels or otherwise. They were members of the unseen world. Angels were messengers who were responsible to God and had an obligation to give an account to God (Hebrews 1:14). The picture painted by the author points to God's governance of the earth and of the heavens. The author is screaming for all to hear: GOD IS IN CHARGE.

God's control is expressed in the question to Satan: *have you considered my servant Job* (1:8; 2:3)? Although the question does not imply that no other creatures were to be considered, God wanted Job to be the main focus. He was the "poster-boy" for God's protection — His love, mercy, and intimacy. He was God's and God was Job's. Foremost, the scene emphasizes God's ownership of creation and all creatures in the seen and unseen worlds and their creaturely dependence on Him. It as if the author of the book made a concerted effort from the outset to depict God as number One!

The idea expressed in the words *present themselves* indicate that ministers and representatives appeared before the king as pictured in Ahab's court (1 Kings 22:9-29 especially verse 19). The scene recorded in the first two chapter of the book of Job is for mankind's and the reader's benefit. It pictures God meeting with members of His council as He presided over His creation and conducted the affairs of the world. The members of the council were correctly interested in what was happening in God's world. Satan's interest flowed from rebellious, ignorant arrogance. The author placed God, the host of heaven and earth, in His place of honor, authority, and power. The attendees were in their place of subordination. The scene is best interpreted as prophetic and even parabolic. God is in His heaven and words must be few but true and reverent (Ecclesiastes 5:2). Satan had not and will never learn that lesson.

Satan was present as an agent of the Lord (see Jeremiah 25:9, 27:6; 43:10; Isaiah 44:24-45:3: Nebuchadnezzar and Cyrus were described as God's servants). Satan was depicted as the only one who conversed with God. In God's presence Satan's words were many and disrespectful. Yet he lived which was in contrast to the teaching in the Old Testament that seeing God's face or being in God's presence — brought death (Genesis 16:13; 32:30; 33:20; Exodus 33:20, 23)!

In the first two chapters, the author goes to great lengths to emphasize the fact of God's control. Not only does the reader meet Job in these chapters, but more so, the reader meets a sovereign God in control of the heavens, the earth, and all creatures. The world is His and everything in it (Psalms 24:1-2; 29:1-11; 33:6-11; 50:8-13). God's sovereign plan began in eternity, took shape in the council of heaven, and unfolded in time and space on earth. As a result, God's will is accomplished in heaven and is being done on earth. The covenantally faithful God is true to His promises. He is the ultimate Promisemaker and Promisekeeper. These truths initially were a burden for Job; in the end there were one of his greatest blessings.

Application

1. Consider how the author presented God as Controller and Sustainer. What is your response?

2. What is the parallel between 1 Kings 22:9-29 and Job 1:6-12 and 2:1-6?

3. *God is in heaven and all is right with the world, let your words be few* (Ecclesiastes 5:2, see Job 6:24) and Psalm 100:3: *Know that the Lord is God; it is he who made us and we are his; we are the sheep of his pasture*:

   a. What significance do these facts have in your life?

   b. In what ways will you change your thoughts and desires about God and yourself?

   c. How does the reality of God's existence fit with the opening statement of the Lord's Prayer (*Our Father who are in heaven*) . . . ?

CHAPTER 2

God's Control and God's Challenge

Job 1 and 2

GOD GAVE A DECLARATION OF Himself while in council as recorded Job 1:6-12 and 2:1-6. He specifically asked Satan: *Have you considered my servant Job? There is no one on earth like him . . .* (1:8; 2:3)? What a provocative question and declaration! God was setting up Satan! Notice the possessive *my*. God claims Job as His. Satan takes aim at God through Job. Such was Satan's tactic in the wilderness with Christ (Matthew 4 and Luke 4) and with the nation of Israel (Deuteronomy 7:9-12).

In the original language, God used the term *considered* which carries the meaning of *giving over to* and *sober cognition of a person or thing*. The question and the term used by the Holy Spirit indicated that Satan is a rational, thinking being. The question was designed to put Satan on the spot. God was in control.

God added an epitaph. God gave His assessment of Job and simultaneously He made a statement about Himself. God attested to His own activity as Redeemer, Deliverer, Provider, and Sustainer. Job was His child. Moreover, in the heavens God described Job's Christlikeness — Job feared God and shunned evil (1:1, 8; 2:3). These were words of high praise, not only of Job, but more so of God. Job was a product of saving and enabling grace. Job was and would always be a "trophy" of God's care and grace. God offered Job as evidence of His care of His people. However, God knew that the full reality of His work in Job would not become clear to Job until chapters 40 and 42. Job would not fail because God does not fail. One may consider chapters 40 and 42 as a prelude to Pentecost.

By God's design, Satan took the challenge. He responded by presenting his view of Job's alleged holiness, blamelessness, and Christlikeness. By his retort, Satan accused God. He alleged that God had bought Job (1:9-12). Satan was less interested in Job. He wanted to use Job against God. This was a driving motivation in the temptation of Christ in the desert/wilderness (Matthew 4 and Luke 4). Satan wanted to prove God and Christ covenantally unfaithful, losers, and liars.

Satan challenged God to stretch out His hand against Job and strike everything he had (Job 1:11). How interesting that Satan appealed to God's sovereign power and control. The word translated stretch refers to *send out, send away,* or *to extend*. It refers to influence and control. Satan challenged God to remove His control — His protection and blessings from Job.

By God's creative design man is a chooser and a worshipping being. Job was a dependent being in God's world. Job was in covenant with God because God was in covenant with him. Satan wanted to break that relationship. Satan reasoned that Job's sinful response to God's withdrawal of blessings would demonstrate to God, to Job, and to the world, the truth about God and Job. Satan was sure the *real God* would be demonstrated for Who He was and how He did things. Satan's challenge to God focused on Job's choice to be a God-pleaser or self–pleaser. This was Satan's tactic in the Garden of Eden, with Christ, and with every believer. Satan desired to discredit God by proving that God used and bought people; if blessings were not forthcoming, Job would stop worshipping God. God would be proved as no better than an idol. Not only would Job be exposed as a fraud, more importantly, God would be exposed as the Fraud! Satan was proclaiming a health-and-wealth gospel and God as the originator of that gospel. The mantra was: *Do God's bidding and earn the prize. Do to get. Focus on self and use God and others.*

Satan's challenge to God was exactly what God intended. A similar scenario would be repeated in the wilderness (Matthew 4; Luke 4). There Satan presented two options to Jesus. Satan hoped to discredit God through Jesus by enticing Him to choose to glorify and please Himself thereby breaking covenant. Jesus would have followed the nation of Israel as a covenant breaker.

Rather Christ was the new Israel and Covenantkeeper. It was simply amazingly miraculous that daily (24/7) and throughout His life, Jesus always chose to please the Father (John 4:31-34). Satan failed miserably in His quest to discredit God and he will continue to fail. Yet he keeps trying. Every Christian daily faces the same challenge and choice of pleasing God for His sake or pleasing self for the sake and glory of the person. The challenge will continue until Christ returns (Romans 12:1-2; 2 Corinthians 5:9; Galatians 5:16-18; 1 John 2:15-17).

Salvation does not immunize the Christian against trouble (life, God's providence). Trouble per say is a result of the curse and a return to the chaos in evidence on the first day of creation (Genesis 1:2; Romans 5:12-14; 2 Corinthians 4:16-18; John 15:18-21, 16:33). God brought the cosmos and order from chaos. God intends for believers to use trouble (chaos) to develop the fruit of the Spirit and Christlikeness — order and glory (Romans 8:28-29). This truth expressed in Genesis 1 is a major lesson of the cross.

God's control was further demonstrated by His restrictions on Satan. He gave specific instructions to Satan in regards to Job. Satan could not affect his body. Job's salvation was not at stake. Rather, God was on trial: His essence and His reputation as a loving, gracious, caring God and Father. Was God who He claimed to be? Moreover, the challenge reached cosmic heights. A cosmic war was unfolding in the earth below! Was God the good and great Lord of lords and King of kings in both the unseen and seen worlds? How would God fare before the whole world? Satan prophesied that Job would *curse* God if enough pressure was applied to him (1:11; 2:5).

Application

1. What do you learn about God?
2. What do you learn about Satan?
3. What do you learn about Job?
4. What do you learn about yourself?

CHAPTER 3

God's Control and His Challenge, Continued

Job 1 and 2

IT IS INTERESTING THAT THE author emphasized Job's concern for his children. Job wondered if they had sinned and if they had cursed God in their hearts (1:5). It is important to note that Satan predicted that Job would curse God.

In offering sacrifices for his children Job served as priest. As noted earlier, Job's activity preceded the giving of the Ten Commandments and specifically the Third Commandment. Satan claimed that Job would curse God and profane His name when God pressured Job (1:9-11; 2:4-6). Job's wife counseled Job to curse God as trouble mounted for Job and her (Job 2:9; 5:7; 14:1). Sarcastically, Satan *informed* God that all the sacrifices that Job offered for his kids should have been offered for Job!

The word *curse* is the same word for the counsel his wife gave Job in 2:9. She told her husband to *curse* God and die. Unwittingly we hope, she urged her husband to follow Satan's prediction. The word translated as *curse* is the common term *barak* which most often is translated as *blessing*. Some speculate the word was used as a euphemism to avoid the thought that someone would actually curse God.

According to Satan, proof that God was or was not a liar and a fraud rested upon Job's response to God's previous providence. Initially God blessed Job as He did Noah with prosperity: family, children, friends, and material possessions. Both were in covenant with God and God with them. For the average person, especially an Israelite, wealth and prosperity were signs of God's approval. Loss of them was a sign of His disapproval. Job was in a quandary. People thought about him as many did Jesus: both were losers! Their hard times proved that fact.

Job faced trouble as another aspect of God's providence. In this way Job was a type of Christ. Jesus and Job experienced trouble and hard times which was not of their own sin. The question before both was their faithfulness: was it to God and His promises or to self and their own wisdom. Ignorantly, initially, Job made the issue God's faithfulness and his vindication.

Satan was God's active agent as was Cyrus and Nebuchadnezzar (Isaiah 44:24-45:3; Jeremiah. 25:9; 27:6; 43:10). Initially, Satan's activity was restricted to activities outside of Job (1:13-19). Job did not follow Satan's prediction. In response and in accordance with God's sovereign plan, Satan upped the stakes. The second round of the *seeming* trial of Job was intended to be God's trial. Arrogantly and ignorantly Satan pressed the issue! He declared that if God affected the person of Job directly, Job would curse God (2:4-5).

From Satan's perspective he had God and Job right where he wanted them. Subsequently Job was affected by a wasting disease as described in Exodus 9:9-11. His body was under attack but his whole person was involved — thoughts, desires, and actions. This latter fact is so often missed. Too often there is a tendency to dichotomize man by speaking of him as a duality — body and soul. As such, those who approach man from this perspective will address the body and the soul or inner man independently. Rather man is a duplex, united whole person and both aspects of him must be approached theologically together! These facts mean that the outer- and inner-man are linked. Further, it means that thoughts, desires, and actions occur in both the outer- and inner-man and influence the whole person. The whole person acts! Therefore, the whole person must be addressed. I will revisit this vital ministry point.

Job experienced God's providence through a series of events including hard times which seems to be an understatement. To Job and his wife, it was as though all the forces of heaven and earth were conspiring against Job. His initial responses to God's providence were noteworthy.

First, Job lost animals, servants, and family (1:13-19). Verse 22 recorded Job's response: *In all this, Job did not charge God with wrong doing.* The term in the original language translated as *charge* is used over 2000 times in the Old Testament. It carries the meaning *to put, to give,* or *to place.* In this context, the word carried a judicial overtone. At this point, Job did not charge God with any wrongdoing. The judicial aspect of Job's response becomes more prominent as events unfold.

Second, Job is afflicted with a devastating skin problem that affected his whole body (2:7-8; Exodus 9:9-11). His wife gave him satanic counsel: . . . *curse God and die* (2:9). Job's wife was another of God's agents. Her counsel would have Job follow Satan's prediction (2:5). Job's wife is not mentioned again in the book. Tradition believes that Job's wife may have been Dinah, the daughter of Jacob or one of Dinah's daughters. We are not told her motivation in giving Job this counsel. God does not rebuke her or have Job offer sacrifices for her as Job did for the three friends (42:7ff). In the end, Job was blessed with more children and we suspect by the same wife (42:13-15).

The world of Job and his wife had been radically changed. Their theology came to the fore. Such it is in times of trouble. The author of Proverbs knew heart exposure occurred in both hard and easy times and he asked for neither riches nor poverty (Proverbs 30:7-9). Hard times (God's providence), but also "easier" times (also God's providence), are the context in which a person demonstrates the significance of his relationship with the Lord. In the Synoptic gospels (Matthew 19:16-27; Mark 10:17-30; Luke 18:18-30), each writer records Jesus' encounter with the rich young ruler. One aspect of the story is pertinent to Job. Unlike Job the ruler had a high view of himself and his lawkeeping. Perhaps he had a low view of God, holiness, and perfect lawkeeping. But he had wealth which the apostles and the people considered a sign of God's favor. Jesus called for the ruler to divorce himself from his self as manifested by his demand to have things. Jesus told him to change his allegiance from himself and things to Him. He refused. In response, the apostles wanted to know who could be saved. They understood, wrongly, that "stuff" is proof-positive of God's favor. Jesus disabused them of this fact. God may grant material things and prosperity to some, but poverty or wealth may be a sign of blessing or cursing. Both are always a matter of testing (Deuteronomy 8). God gives, and He withholds for His own purposes, but it is always for His glory and the believer's good. Job would have to learn this lesson in God's classroom.

God's providence is an expression of God's purposeful love, power, and authority for all creatures especially for His people. Hard or "easy" providences do not necessarily indicate the significance of God's relationship to the person as if God has targeted the person (consider Christ and the cross, Job, John 9; 2 Corinthians 12:7-10). Moreover, the believer will experience the fullness of the depth of the riches of God's relational love (Ephesians 3:13-19). Job was to experience the bliss of heaven in the midst of hard times. Initially, he vigorously denied that fact.

God's providence is the crucible for refining the believer The believer is faced with circumstances outside of his control but so ordered by God. He is to use them to grow in Christlikeness. Otherwise he will respond according to satanic reasoning and logic, thus becoming more like him (Romans 8:28-29; James 1:2-4; 1 Peter 1:6-7). This truth that God is working for good is sometimes simply a platitude given to people because we can't understand God. However, it is a truth that was radically displayed at the cross. On the cross and even before, God's glory was being manifested in the person of Christ. The cross "digs" into and exposes the depths of the Triune God's wisdom, love, and power. God's providence, especially hard ones, tend to draw out functional unbelief and expose the believer's heart. For the believer, it is meant to prune and refine.

God squeezes the heart of every person so that the contents of the heart in terms of loyalty, allegiance, and devotion become manifest. Pressure — God's providence — can be used for good by the believer if it is used properly. Good is defined as growth in Christlikeness. A proper understanding of God, self, others, and providence leads to a proper response to God and His providence and vice versa. A proper response is likened to the formation of a pearl of Christlikeness as the oyster responds to and uses irritation to form a pearl. The world of nature and the oyster has a lesson for the believer. The believer is to use irritations — hard times — to make the pearl of Christlikeness (Romans 8:28-29; 2 Corinthians 5:9).

Job gave a wonderful answer to his wife: *how can we accept good from God and not trouble. In all this, Job did not sin in what he said* (2:10). The term translated *trouble* is a very common and generic word used about 350 times in the Old Testament. It is translated as bad, evil, misery, and distress. It includes trouble in a general sense and can refer to spiritual and physical problems. It is another term for God's providence. Job acknowledged God as the Giver of all things. Job knew that his situation could not determine his response to God and His providence. Job acknowledged himself in particular and man in general as the recipient from God's hand and he taught his wife the *how* of godly receiving.

As we move through the book you must remember the words recorded in Job 1:22 and 2:10 and the presence and silence of the three friends (2:11-13). Those passages present Job as someone who did not sin when initially faced with God's sovereign control and the false counsel of his wife. The three friends committed themselves to comforting Job which they did initially. However, things changed as Job faced his three friends and their counsel rather than simply their presence. Eventually Job made demands upon God. God owed him!

Again, I repeat, an outstanding fact for correctly interpreting the book of Job is Job's exceptional relationship with God and God with Job. God Himself said as much (1:1, 3, 8; 2:3). Job knew God or at least he thought he did. He knew as well as any spiritually mature person can. More importantly, he would discover that

God knew him better than he knew himself and he knew God. He knew he was God's but doubted the significance of that fact as he continued *under the circumstances*. He began to live the lie.

Circumstances did not negate the truth that God is God and every believer is a child of God. As such, intimacy with God is constant even though feelings, human understanding divorced from biblical truth, experience, and circumstances may suggest otherwise. Job had enjoyed God and fellowship with Him. He was confident in that relationship and he was confident in God. One may say that their relationship was "tight." Again, in this sense, Job was a type of Christ. These facts take on more significance as we move through the book. Job was aghast that seemingly his relationship meant so little to God as evidenced by his condition.

Application

1. As far as Job was concerned, God's control and power was never the question. What became the question and even a demand?

2. Job was not aware of chapters 1 and 2 — the activity in the unseen world. What was Job to rely upon as one of God's creatures?

3. Job's wife is not mentioned again in the book. What motivated her to give that counsel and how is it similar to Satan's counsel in the Garden (see Genesis 3)?

CHAPTER 4

Job's Initial Response: Part 1

Job 3

CHAPTERS 3-31 CONTAIN JOB'S OPENING monologue (Job 3), the counsel of the friends, and Job's responses to each of his friends. The various dialogues contain an interesting array of thoughts, misunderstandings, desires, demands, and concerns. The counsel of the three friends is based on a wrong view of man, and more so, a wrong view of God and His ways. As a result, there is confusion and dissatisfaction for all involved. Initially, God is not honored even though each player professes to be seeking to aid Job and to speak truth. Each of the friends articulated his version of wisdom which only added to Job's burden. Each proclaimed their view of how God works in His world. However, neither of the friends asked Job any questions! They did not seek to learn God's perspective in order to give the most appropriate and relevant truth for Job in his situation given his spiritual maturity and his willingness to hear and assimilate it. They simply began to speak.

The chapters include a mantra of suggestions for Job based on the standard of experience, mystical or otherwise, and dreams (Eliphaz), tradition (Bildad), and human knowledge apart from biblical truth (Zophar). We assume that each person believed that the truth will set one free. But they failed to consider that falsehood imprisons a person. Job was "drowning" and the counsel of his friends only added to his burden. However, Job's "drowning" was part of his own making based on his wrong view of God and his problem which directed his response.

In the end, Job repented and was restored. The three friends were confronted by God for their faulty counsel that was based on wrong views of God. Job interceded for them and they were not consumed. God's truth was needed which came only after Job entered into God's presence completely silent (Job 38-42). He had demanded God to speak. God flooded Job with wisdom, power, might, majesty, and goodness. Job was mesmerized, awe-struck, and silent. He eventually repented (Job 42:6)!

We must remember that through it all Job had an overriding concern. Job as well as his three friends never doubted God's sovereignty. The three friends wanted Job to repent. Job wanted clarification that his relationship with God was intact. He wanted assurance that God's covenantal relationship with him and his with God was not in jeopardy. It seemed to him and the others that there was a relational problem between God and Job. The three friends interpreted Job's circumstances according to the common theology of the day which led them to their conclusions about Job's problem and solution. The theology espoused by the friends is summarized as the law of retribution as discussed earlier: bad things happen to people who deserve them and repentance is the way out of bad circumstances. In their scheme God's grace and mercy were lacking. God's justice and wrath is expressed due to covenant breaking but the friends had a faulty view of God's covenant promises. Repentance was a tool to get from God. This theology eviscerates the cross. It makes Jesus a loser and sinner.

This theology continued to be prominent in Jesus' day (Luke 13:1-5; John 9). It is still relevant today which leads to a wrong understanding of such passages as Matthew 8:17 and Isaiah 53:3-6. These passages refer to Jesus' redemptive once-for-all substitutionary sacrifice. They do not refer to the removal of the curse of sin on the body in this life (Romans 5:12-14). Some interpret Matthew 8:17 to mean that faith is the key for "physical healing", a type of health-wealth gospel. The more faith one can generate the less problems he or she has and the more healing one is alleged to receive. The person is caught up in a cycle of *more belief* for the sake of self and fewer problems.

Some believe that Isaiah 53 refers to Jesus' culpability — He was not the sinless Sin-bearer. However, Jesus was and is the impeccable One (Hebrews 4:15; 7:26; 9:28; 1 Peter 2:22-24; 1 John 3:5). He had no sin and He did not sin. Therefore, He left heaven, lived a perfect life, went to the cross, and died a perfect death but not for His *own* sin (Romans 3:21-26; 2 Corinthians 5:21). Rather, He lived perfectly, and He died perfectly for His people, their guilt and condemnation.

Job wanted confirmation that God's relationship with him was still intact even though it appeared that God had broken fellowship with him. His circumstances seem to have indicated this fact. However, Job knew his relationship with God had been grounded in fear of the Lord and not in merit from good deeds or more faith. As did Abraham, Job had some understanding of the doctrine of justification by faith (Genesis 15:6; Galatians 3:6, 8). This aspect of his theology was solid as God Himself acknowledged (Job 1:1, 8; 2:3). However, Job lacked a full understanding and personal application of the gospel truth termed justification by faith alone which is through Christ by grace alone via the Holy Spirit. As the trouble (God's providence) persisted and Job's condition became increasingly unpleasant, the theological pundits continued to voice misleading counsel. In response to them and God's seeming silence and apathy, Job became increasingly dissatisfied. He wanted complete and even immediate clarity regarding his relationship with God and his future.

His friends did not shed any light on God's answer because they did not have a proper theology. Their initial presence and silence could be termed a ministry. Their presence and silence had been a blessing and comfort but their counsel was a burden because it was wrong and continuous. They misrepresented God, Job, and themselves. When Job did not get a satisfactory answer from his friends, he demanded an answer from God. Moreover, as we shall see, he took God to court. He was sure he had been treated unfairly by God (30:24). In the end, Job repented and he agreed with God. The friends were correct: Job needed to repent but not for the reasons based on their faulty "wisdom." Job reevaluated himself and God and found himself wanting. However, the three friends failed to repent. They did not bless Job, but God mercifully had Job intercede for them! God through Job blessed them even though God agreed that the three friends had missed the mark (Job 42:7-9). I suspect that at some point they did repent due to the mercy of God and the graciousness of Job. God also ministered to Job who also had it wrong about himself and God (Job 40:3-5; 42:4-6). Only God had it correct! But, He never left Job or the three friends.

Job sought knowledge and assurance. He wanted answers. He wanted to know what God was doing and why. He wanted to hope and trust, but Job wanted to know first. His understanding must be satisfied. Faith and trust took a backseat. Job was in an anti-Augustine and anti-Anselm posture: knowing came before believing and trusting rather than *faith seeks understanding* and *faith on a quest to know.* For Job, knowing why was the key. Trusting and honoring God was a distance second.

The link between faith and knowledge is another major theme of the book of Job. Man is faith-based and a thinking being. Therefore, faith always seeks knowledge and knowledge always seeks faith in order to put on more faithfulness. Faith and knowledge are not to be divorced.

Job was faced with a choice as are all believers: to know and trust based on some standard: God's or the person's (Proverbs 3:5-8). From Job's perspective at least initially, his hope was death (3:1-26; 19:25-27). Initially and throughout, Job did not hope and trust as he should and could have. Again, he lived the lie. He eventually demanded an audience with God which he received (Job 38-42). When confronted with God and truth, Job shut his mouth until he confessed and repented. He was not as wise as he thought!

Application

1. Truth sets a person free and falsehood imprisons:

   a. What was the source of the three friends counsel and truth?

   b. Summarize their theology and their solution.

2. What was the theology of the day and how would it explain Jesus and the cross?

3. What Job's was a major concern?

4. How did the friends address his concern?

CHAPTER 5

Job's Initial Response: Part II

Job 3

CHAPTER 3 OPENS WITH: *AFTER this, Job opened his mouth and cursed the day of his birth* (3:1). Job claimed that he can no longer testify that life is God's good gift and expressed the desire to leave creation behind (3:1-26). He opted out for the primordial chaos. The word translated as *curse* in verse 1 (*barak*: see page 31) emphasizes the absence or reversal of a blessed estate or moving to a lower and less blessed position or state. It describes the results of a decision. Job underscored his view of his predicament by the understatement: *I am miserable.*

Job's existence which had been a joy to him was now a burden (3:2-3). He desired relief — he wanted out (3:5-7). He voiced the thought that if he had not been born he would be at rest (3:11-13). In verses 11-19, Job moved from lamenting and cursing his birth (v.1-10) to questioning why he been born. He questioned why he didn't die at birth. He desired to never have been conceived, never to have been born, and once born to have died. In 1:10, Satan attempted to use God's *hedge* (*sakal*: 1:9: protection and care of Job) against God, and in 3:23, Job perceived the hedging action of God as a burden/restriction. What Satan labeled as protection Job viewed as a burden. He lamented that he had no shalom: no peace, quietness, or rest; he had only turmoil (verses 13, 17, 26).

Job had lost possessions and family. His whole body was covered with open sores. In God's providence, Job's problems were initially external (1:13-19) and then his body was directly affected (2:7-8). God had "turned up the heat." He was hardly recognizable to his friends (2:11-13). Job was stunned and confused. Here and throughout the book, Job did not deny that God was at work. He knew that God ordains all that comes to pass. The key for him was *why* in relational terms. Job, initially, was asking, and then demanded to know: *What* is God doing and *why* is He doing it since I have a good relationship with Him?

Again, for Job, relationships mattered. This man of God had been placed in a woeful, heart-wrenching situation by God. It forced him to think vertically. Initially before the events of God's providence as described in chapters 1-2, he had the correct orientation and reference which was properly Godward. Now, in the middle of unpleasantness, he expressed confusion in very definite terms. Some may say that Job hit "rock-bottom" or hit the bottom of a pit (see Jeremiah 20:14-18 which is a paraphrase of Job 3:3-19. Jeremiah reconsidered his commission as God's prophet. Like Job, he sunk from a position of exaltation to the depths of hopelessness). Both Job's and Jeremiah's thinking was along these lines: God has made a mistake — *the hole is too deep, the mountain too high, and the tunnel so long and dark.* Both Job and Jeremiah were on the verge of living the lie. As we shall see, God had Job, and Jeremiah, right where He wanted them.

Some may say that Jesus also hit "rock-bottom" in the Garden the night before He went to the cross (Matthew 26:36-46; Mark 14:32-42; Luke 22:40-46). I don't think that was the case at all. In the Garden Jesus poured out Himself and His blood to the Father (see Luke's account) before He shed His blood before the world. Jesus understood the beginning and the end and all in between. Jesus' humiliation occurred the moment He left heaven and took on human flesh (at the Incarnation) which was long before the cross itself. The cross was truly His destiny on earth, but it was for His own glory and exaltation, for the glory of the Triune God, and for the saving of His people (John 17:1-5, 24-26; Hebrews 12:1-3; Philippians 2:9-11). What held Jesus to His mission and ministry was His singular motivation of glorifying the Triune God by pleasing His Father and completing His Messiahship on earth (John 4:31-34; Hebrews 12:1-3). He viewed circumstances through a biblical grid and not God and His purposes through circumstances. Jesus bids all His children to do the same. Job eventually learned the lesson that Jesus demonstrated at the cross (1 Corinthians 1:18f). Along the way

Jesus was tempted with false counsel by Satan, the people, and His own disciples (Matthew 4 and Luke 4; John 2:24-25; Matthew 16:21-23). Jesus chose the wisdom of God.

Job had faulty reasoning as did his friends. His understanding and the logic of the day as it was presented by his friends only confused the issue. Job and the three friends would never understand the cross and Jesus' ministry if Job and the three friends continued to rely on their own understanding. We know that Job became a wise man (42:2-6). We are not told how the three friends responded after their encounter with God (Job 42).

Retuning to chapter 3, Job condemned the day of his birth in verse 10. He then asked a series of rhetorical *why* questions beginning with why he did not perish at birth (3:11-23). Yet, Job knew his birth and his situation was part of God's providence. His three friends and their misleading, short-sighted counsel was also part of God's providence. Job presented the view that non-birth was better than his present life (3:1-3). As the book progressed, Job's continued misery only strengthened his initial assessment: non-birth was preferable. He demanded a response from God. Eventually after an encounter with God, Job retracted those words and changed his mindset (see Job 40 and 42).

The book of Job does not say that Job ceased to trust God or that he cursed God. Job did accuse and charge God. Many would say his circumstances "made him do it" or made it "Okay" for him to think and act in a certain way. Moreover, Job would declare that the counsel of the three friends only added to his burden (Job 16:2). Our psychologized culture would declare Job a victim, a sad case, and not responsible. However, the Bible does not teach that God's providence in any form is a cause or the reason for a person's sinful response to Him and to others. Interestingly, initially Job responded to his wife in a loving, wise manner (2:9-10). However, Job changed as he continued with his problems and ungodly counsel. It was as if he became comfortable living the lie.

I repeat: God's providence is the context for the person's response. It exposes the inner man. A response to events and people is a response to God. In chapters 40 and 42, God brought Job to his knees by bringing him to Himself. But Job brought himself to his knees. Job humbled himself (James 4:6-10; 1 Peter 5:6-10). God had not left Job even though Job considered God's presence a burden (Job 3:26; 23:2; 33:7-11).

Please note as I repeat an important truth: Job's humiliation did not humble him. Humiliation refers to the situation and context — God's providence. I will return to this important but often neglected point. Humbling oneself is what a person does by the agency of the Holy Spirit through enabling grace in the context of the believer's relationship with Christ. Contrary to Satan's prediction, Job eventually became a humble, wise, and grateful man of God (see Job 40 and 42). Job grew and God was glorified.

However, prior to evidence of his growth, Job took God to court! God said as much in Job 40:2 (also see 13:3, 6; 16:21; 19:6; 31:35). The question: what did Job accuse and charge God with and did he curse God? Did the devil win (Genesis 3:15; Romans 16:20; Colossians 2:13-15; Hebrews 2:14; 1 John 3:8)? Is it possible for the devil, the antithesis of the Triune God, a created being, and a minion of God to win? The answer is a resounding NO! Early on Job had functionally reversed the Creator-creature distinction. He began to function as if God owed him. As is evident in Chapters 38-42, God disabused Job of himself and this mindset. Job became a wise man. The Holy Spirit teaches in and throughout the book that God is the Winner and believers share in that victory as more than conquerors (Romans 8:35-39). Satan did not and will not win. He and those in his family and kingdom are the losers (Genesis 3:15; Romans 16:20; 1 John 3:8; Revelation 22:12-21)!

Application

1. Read chapter 3 and catch a glimpse of Job's initial response.

   a. What is your reaction?

   b. What is the Holy Spirit's message?

2. Do you think Job would have responded as he did if he had been aware of the events documented in the first two chapters?

3. Anticipate God's final answer for Job. Write it out and review it at the end of the book.

CHAPTER 6

Job's Initial Response: Part III

Job 3

THE LAST SEVEN VERSES OF chapter 3 (v.20-26) give an interesting outlook. Job acknowledged that he had been born and survived until the days of his "hard times." Death seemed preferable to his God-given situation. Sadly, this is a typical response for both believers and unbelievers especially when faced with any trouble but most often "heavy trouble." Yet I contend that the degree of Job's angst was intensified by his desire to "figure God out" and to know the end. It will become clear that Job wanted to walk by sight rather than saving faith (Romans 8:24-25; 2 Corinthians 5:7, 9). As mentioned, Job wanted understanding more than faithfulness. Actually, Job wanted God to supply him a reason for his condition. He wanted God to explain Himself. He had faith and he had knowledge. The issue was being a good steward of both by focusing on God as He is. Job was far too concerned with the *why* of God's ways. Job's own reasoning was his standard and guide for "figuring out" God. His ways determined his response.

At the crux of Job's angst and inner-man turmoil was his demand for a true, comprehensive knowledge of God and His care in the context of hard times. Job wanted to know why, not the God of the why. In the end, Job came to know the God of the why and not the why. The fact that he was thrilled is an understatement (Job 40, 42).

As I have said Job was a type of Jesus. However, Jesus knew His beginning — His origin, His end — His destiny, and the middle — His identity and purpose. As do all believers, Job knew his origin, his identity, his purpose, and his destiny because he was saved. Yet he did not know Christ and himself as he ought. Believers are to imitate Christ and become more like Christ this side of heaven. These facts are more vivid and clear for believers on this side of the cross. However, no matter which side of the cross, believers, including Job, are to imitate Christ who kept His gaze on the big picture and the end result. Christ's relationship with the Father and His desire to glorify Him by pleasing Him carried the Jesus all the way to the cross and beyond (Hebrews 12:1-3; John 4:31-34; 6:37-43). So it is for all believers in every age. Job came to know and experience this truth (Job 42). A major teaching point in the book of Job is the simple fact that circumstances must be seen through the eyes of saving faith coupled with a proper understanding of God and self, both of which are directed toward glorifying a powerful, good, and trustworthy God.

Initially, Job missed the significance of a proper relationship with God. He wanted to know what was going on between God and him. He wanted to know the significance of relationships and he wanted to know why he was being treated the way he was. Job's situation raised several questions for him and all believers one of which is captured in the question: how can anyone be sure of the significance of God's relationship with him if Job did not? Satan reasoned and would have all people reason: *bad times are proof that something was not right with God. God could not keep His people safe.* If this statement is true, then Jesus was a loser and fraud.

Job 3:23 gives an insight into Job: *Why is life given to a man whose way is hidden and God has hedged in?* As I have mentioned, in 1:10, Satan attempted to use God's hedge (see 1:9: protection and care of Job) against God. Satan charged God with providing protection for Job and thus earning *goodies* and *brownie points* with Job. In essence, Satan charged that God had bought Job. In verse 23, Job is tacitly agreeing with Satan. Satan totally and Job partially did not understand the atonement - buying back by paying the ransom price (Romans 3:21-26). God buys His people but through the blood of Christ, the true Lamb! The price is paid in full!

Job was ignorant as was Satan. In Job 3:23, Job said that God's presence and His hedging action was a burden, a restriction whereas Satan called it a protection, a safety net (1:10). Given his situation, Job did not appreciate God's presence. As the book unfolds Job demanded God to speak and he desired to be in His presence. One wonders if Job knew what he was demanding and from Whom. Was he demanding an answer as the creature to the Creator and Controller or was he seeking a personal interview with God in order to serve his God? Early on Job functioned as if he had a right to make a claim on God.

God's presence and His previous gifts were now pictured as oppressive (Job 3:23-26; see also 23:2; 3:7-11; see David's response in Psalm 32 and 38). Job could not figure out God! In David's case he had unconfessed sin. Job had no such thing. Job did not appreciate or *feel* God's presence; he declared that God seemed to be nowhere. Job lived the lie and I suspect he "knew better" (Psalms 24:1-2; 50:8-13; 139:1-12). Job expressed this thought even though he knew God was in control. Trust and obedience are twin pillars for the believer that flow from a correct view of God and that He is at work in all things working them for His glory and the good of His people (Genesis 50:15-21; Romans 8:28-29). God is completely sovereign, infinite in wisdom, and perfect in love. Therefore, God knows what is best, wills what is best, and brings to pass what is best for himself and His people (Jerry Bridges, *Trusting God When Life Hurts*, Nav Press, 1988, page 18). That is "heavy" theology! However, it sustained Christ and, in the end, it sustained Job. It will sustain you, believer, but proper theology is to be applied properly!

God's seeming silence and hidden presence were a burden for Job. God is the Hedger (Protector) par excellence, but Job needed an educative and humbling lesson on who God is and how He works. Job 9:5-10 is a marvelous hymn about God's presence and His greatness but Job was not initially blessed by them. Similarly, in Job 38-41, God used creation to demonstrate His good and marvelous control. Initially, Job did not connect God's creative and sustaining power with God's wisdom and mercy. Job was not blessed by God's presence, power, and control. However, chapters 40 and 42 recorded Job's about face — he got it! God did not change — Job did! We all need to get it!

In the end unlike Christ (remember Job is a type of Christ), Job confessed and repented (chapters 40 and 42). In the closing chapters, God gave Job Himself in a way that this man of God had never known (Psalm 34:8; Philippians 3:7-11). Job never knew of God's encounter with Satan. Moreover, Job failed to view things from a cosmic perspective with God as Father and Head, Creator, and Controller of all creation. After God's encounter with Job, Job was overwhelmingly satisfied with God for who He was and for the fact that his relationship with this personal, powerful God was intact. This occurred before he was restored physically and materially!

Job did not get an explanation of why God works in His world in the way He does (Genesis 50:19-21; Romans 8:28-

29). What Job received after a personal encounter with the living God was God Himself in greater fullness. Job did not get answers to his questions. He got God because God always had him. As he had moved toward God, he was able to leave his questions behind!

Application

1. What is your view of relationships?
2. What is your view of God's relationship with you and yours to Him?

    a. What is the basis of that relationship? John 3:3-8

    b. On earth, what is to happen after salvation? 2 Corinthians 5:9, 14-15; Titus 2:11-14
3. How has the fact of God's relationship with you influenced you? Give examples.
4. What is your view of your relationship with God in Christ by the Holy Spirit and how has it changed?
5. How has your relationship with Christ influenced your thoughts, desires, and actions in any circumstance so that you are becoming more like Christ daily?

CHAPTER 7

The Speeches of the Three Friends: Part I

CHAPTER 3 IS FOLLOWED BY the speeches of Job's friends in response to Job and his condition: Eliphaz (chapters 4-5, 15, 22); Bildad (chapters 8, 18, 25); and Zophar (chapters 11, 20). Each friend traced Job's trouble to personal sins including cruelty to the widow and the fatherless (4:7; 8:20; 11:6; 22:5-10). Notice that the speeches were shorter as the book progressed and Zophar gave only two speeches. In spite of their initial silent vigil with Job (2:11-13), the friends failed to gather information from Job before they offered their solution. They failed to learn Job's perspective and consequently they failed to meet Job with God's truth that was most applicable to Job in his situation given his theological maturity and willingness to hear. In fact, the three friends had a limited and incorrect fund of knowledge to bring to Job, but they denied that fact.

As one reads their reasoning and counsel, it is apparent that they considered Job's problem apart from him as a person and his relationship with God. In fact, they filtered Job's experience through their own understanding of God as judged by the classical standards of feelings, experience, tradition, and human understanding. Based on their understanding and the law of retribution, they reasoned that they had no problems, but Job did. Therefore, Job should repent but not them. They believed they had no reason to repent but Job had every reason to repent. Repentance was the means for restoration — to get. Their line of reasoning had no place for God's mercy and grace. Moreover, it eviscerates the cause of Christ and the cross. In fact, they would have seen no reason for the cross. Faced with Jesus and the cross, they would have considered that Jesus must have done something wrong or He would not be in trouble. A person's relationship with God in Christ was envisioned as a means to get.

The goal of every counselor — everyone is a counselor as well as a counselee — is to present the most relevant biblical truth that is most appropriate for the person in his situation given his degree of willingness and spiritual maturity. As I said above the friends failed to learn Job's thoughts and desires by asking appropriate questions. Rather, they gave their counsel to Job based on their one-sided understanding of God. Their God was easy to figure out. These failures resulted in giving counsel that was based on the belief that one truth fits all people in all circumstances. They spoke at Job rather with him. They boiled God down to a formula. Their arguments were reductionistic. Job must repent because bad things happened to him. He had to be guilty. The circumstances proved it. If and when Job repents God will restore his fortunes. In contrast, as I have written previously, the three friends did not believe they needed to repent because they were not experiencing any bad things. Circumstances proved that fact as well.

In the theology espoused by the three friends, repentance was a tool to get rather than a gift and blessing to be used to honor God. Both Job and the three friends grew weary. They concluded that Job was obstinate and self-righteous. Job concluded that they were wrong. Yet the three friends stayed with Job — initially in silence and then in conversation. Their theology was wrong and so was their solution. God pronounced this fact to them in Chapter 42. If left to themselves and their theology, they would never understand and glory in the cross and the Christ of the cross (Galatians 6:14).

A fair summary of their theology is expressed by Jesus in Luke 13:1-5 and John 9:1-3. Bad things happen to bad people — those who do bad things — or to those whose parents sinned. Punishment and blessings are directly proportional to how good or bad one is. Since Job was having so much trouble, terrible sin must be present in his life, his parents' life, and or in his children's lives. Repentance was the answer and the key to getting back into God's graces. They believed that if trouble came, the key was to repent of something. The three expressed an unspoken corollary: if a person, themselves included, does not have trouble, they have no need to repent.

The three friends viewed and interpreted Job and his circumstances through the grid of their own standards which was God as they knew Him. Interestingly and importantly, neither Job nor the three friends doubted God's control. The issue for all four was never God's control but *why*. For Job, it was relational. What did his relationship to God actually mean? For the three friends, it was relational but in a skewed way. A person's relationship with God is to get and to avoid. One of their major premises — we reap what we sow — was correct. However, a second premise — we reap only what we sow — was false. The cross is the prime example of this truth.

The thoughts expressed in the dialogues of the three friends have a common theme that makes it impossible for anyone to understand, let alone embrace the cross and Christ's mediatorial work. Another summation of their theology follows this line of reasoning: anyone that the world snubs and who experiences "bad things" must be a loser, even a wicked person. "Bad things" don't happen to good people no matter how you define both good and bad. Look at Job and look at them for proof of their correctness. Again, their theology obliterates the true meaning of the cross.

As the Pharisees of Jesus' day, the three friends did not think they needed a spiritual overhaul. Only Job did. They were "OK" (Matthew 5:17-20; 9:12-13; 12:7). To bolster their stance, they pointed to circumstances — Job's and theirs — which proved their point. Therefore, according to them, the only recourse for Job was the work of repentance. The goal was not to glorify or to please God but to get from Him. Properly, Job said whoa!

Application

1. God provided Job with three friends and counselors who were willing to help.

   a. How did they help?

   b. How did they hinder?

   c. What was God's purpose for them?

2. What was their basis for their counsel?

3. How was it reductionistic?

4. What truth did they have?

CHAPTER 8

The Speeches of the
Three Friends: Part II

AS GIVEN IN CHAPTERS 4-5, 15, 22, Eliphaz based his
conclusions on personal observations and experience, often
a mystical one through dreams and his understanding of
how God works (4:8-11, 12-21). Eliphaz gives one source of
wisdom and counsel in 4:8: *As I have observed, those who plow
evil and those who sow trouble reap it* (See Galatians 6:9). His
personal observations and his description and interpretation
of those observations played a major role in his counsel to Job.
Initially, he tried to correctly interpret Job's understanding
of his predicament: *But now trouble comes to you , and you are
discouraged; it strikes you, and you are dismayed* (4:5). But then he
follows with a Pharisaical, works-righteous statement: *Should
not your piety be your confidence and your blameless ways your
hope* (4:6). His question in 4:7 implies a universal, absolute but
abstract principle: *Consider now: Who being innocent ever perished.
Where were the upright ever destroyed?* Eliphaz postulated what
he considered an infallible truth: if Job was truly innocent,
he would never be destroyed. I am sure he meant physically

on this earth because the destiny of everyone is an eternal one — heaven or hell.

For Eliphaz, Job's way out of trouble was his own works-righteousness (4:6). This precept undermined the wisdom and power of God and the cross (Romans 1:16-17; 3:21-26; 4:1-3; 1 Corinthians 1:18-31). After a seemingly gracious start (4:5-6), he concluded that Job was the problem. Based on this theology, Eliphaz had no concept of or need for a suffering Servant and the cross.

In 4:12-21, he emphasized his dependence on dreams and mystical experiences. The conclusion he drew from these experiences was given in verse 17: *Can a mortal be more righteous than God? Can a mortal be more pure than his Creator?* The answer is no. Therefore he concluded that since God is pure and righteous, all mortals are sinful, and God has a right to punish them. This was his answer for the so-called problem of evil. He was correct: God is the just Judge of all the earth and He judges justly (Genesis 18:25; 2 Thessalonians 1:5-10). But he wrongly concluded that all physical problems are evidence of deserved punishment by a righteous God. Eliphaz hinted and insinuated that Job is an evildoer which was the reason for God's punishment (4:7-8). Based on his theology, Eliphaz would *not* have considered himself a loser needing grace.

Eliphaz implied that it was futile to pray to God because Job was resentful toward God (5:1-2). Eliphaz emphasized the earthly destiny of the bad man and the consequences of retribution (5:7; Job agreed, see 14:1). In verses 8-13 and 18-19 of chapter 5, he encouraged Job to go to God *because God catches the wise in their craftiness* (v.13) and *blessed is the man who God disciplines* which is temporary and followed by healing and rescue (v.18). The word *craftiness/crafty* is the word Moses used for the serpent in Genesis 3:1. Eliphaz is indirectly accusing Job of satanic-like thinking.

Eliphaz acknowledged that Job was in a pickle. He gave his reasoning. Job's predicament was due to God's discipline for some unrighteousness in Job and or his family. See Luke 13:1-5 and John 9:1-3. In those verses Jesus encouraged repentance. The fall of Jerusalem in 70 A.D. was looming. Eliphaz ostensibly gave the same answer as Jesus did — which was repentance and turning in humility and confession from sin. However, Jesus was addressing people in a different venue. Eliphaz made repentance a reaction to anyone in any hard times. He would not understand the cross. Moreover, his recommendation applied only to Job and not to Eliphaz himself. In regard to the cross, Eliphaz would agree that Jesus was being disciplined for His own sins. Wow!

Appropriately, Eliphaz attempted to comfort Job. However, his definition of and his manner of comfort was flawed. He tried to motivate Job to repent by such thoughts as: *Blessed is the man whom God corrects . . .* (5:17). Eliphaz told Job that he should be rejoicing and thankful for God's correction (5:17). Assuming he repents, Job would be restored to a favored position. Again, repentance was the means to get.

In chapter 15, Eliphaz sarcastically asked Job if he was God's counselor and had he listened in on God's counsel (15:7-9). In contrast, Paul, in his doxology, and Isaiah used the same question as a blessing (Romans 11:33-35; Isaiah 40:13-14, 28). Paul used this truth to give comfort to Jews and Gentiles who did not understand God's way with ethnic and non-ethnic Israel. Isaiah began the "second portion" of his book (chapters 40-66) with a litany of God's greatness in His wisdom and power as a source of hope for Israel (Isaiah 40:9-31). And in Job 41:11, God used the same formula when speaking to Job as one means of humbling Job. In contrast, Eliphaz used the truth that no one is God's counselor as a hammer to beat up Job. As will be shown, Eliphaz and his friends did not know the mind of Christ (1 Corinthians 2:9-16)!

Eliphaz also rebuked Job because he had moved into the realm of wanting God's knowledge. This in itself was a proper rebuke. However, Eliphaz thought he could explain God and his situation to Job (15:17). Correctly, he insisted that full knowledge was not Job's prerogative. This belonged only to God. In 15:14-16, Eliphaz repeated what he had said in 4:17-19 and what Bildad would say in 25:4-6: God is just and maintains His justice. This is true as far it goes!

Moreover, Eliphaz maintained that God was not apathetic as he thought Job implied. This is also true. He refuted Job's words that God was absent (22:1-3, 12; also see 9:18; 13:24; see Psalm 139). Consequently, Eliphaz's counsel was sprinkled with bits of truth but he failed to portray the true God in His fullness of love and mercy. Retribution via justice and discipline was his key theme but there was no warmth, in part, because there was no mention of God's love and mercy.

Bildad's theology is recorded in chapters 8, 18, 25. His theology is well-stated, neat, analytical, simple, and objective but superficial. He asked Job: *Does God pervert justice? Does the Almighty pervert what is right?* (8:1-3). Bildad accused Job of being a windbag (8:2). According to Bildad it was clear why Job was in trouble and why he, Bildad, was not. Bildad sought his "wisdom" from human tradition calling tradition "former generations" (8:8-10, 11-19; see Galatians 4:3, 9; Colossians 2:8, 20). Bildad told Job that God was punishing him — treating him the way he was — because Job's children sinned and Job was an evildoer (8:4-6, 20). He appealed to his "misunderstanding" of God's justice (8:4-6). All Job had to do was repent. Again, his theology could not explain the cross or bless Job.

Bildad thought he understood God and His ways. He postulated that there are only two kinds of people: the wicked that pervert in secret and the righteous or blameless (v.20-21). Remember, God had proclaimed Job as blameless and righteous (1:1; 2:3). Obviously, Bildad did not agree with God! Bildad postulated that outwardly the two groups appear the same, but God distinguishes them by prospering those who are righteous and punishing those who are wicked — in this life (18:5-21). Bildad concluded that to suggest any other way for God to function doubts God's justice and slanders God as the just Judge of the entire world (Genesis 18:25). Since Job had problems, his only logical recourse was to repent.

For Bildad and Eliphaz, one proof of the validity of their theology was the loss of Job's children (8:4-6; 4:7-8). Job and or his children must have sinned because God's actions match a person's behavior (Luke 13:1-5; John 9:1-3). Moreover, following Bildad's logic, Job's sacrifices for his children must have been a failure (1:5). Chapter 25 consists of only six verses. It is Bildad's feeble attempt to answer Job. Again, he appealed only to God's justice and neglected a full-orbed view of God: His love, mercy, and grace (v. 1-6).

Zophar (chapters 11 and 20) was the least engaging of the three. He claims human knowledge as his standard. He was blunt but interestingly, Zophar's statements (11:7-12) anticipate God's discourses in chapters 38:1-42:6. Believing that Job is not as wise as he claims he asked: *Can you fathom the mysteries of God? Can you probe His limits? They are higher than the heavens — what can you do? They are deeper than the depths of the grave — what can you know?* (v. 7-8; Isaiah 40:28; 55:10-11; Psalms 145:3-7; 147:5).

Correctly, Zophar highlighted the depth, breadth, and height of God's wisdom: It extends beyond the limits of the universe (v.8: sky, underworld, land, and sea). Zophar proclaims: *let me tell you about God's wisdom.* Zophar, seemingly speaking as an expert, is saying that "I can explain Him." He did not think that his rebuke of Job had any relevance for himself!

Like the others he attributed Job's problems to Job's sins (4:7-11; 8:3-6, 20; 11:1-12). Even then, Zophar claimed that God had not punished Job for all of his sins (11:6, 7-11). He began to attack Job based on his interpretation of what Job had said (11:1-20). Zophar wished God would speak to Job thereby putting him in his place (11:5-6). Interestingly, that is exactly what took place as recorded in chapters 38-42!

Like the Pharisees, Zophar did not think God needed to speak to him or that he needed to be "put in his place"! He urged Job to repent which would make it "all right" with God (11:13-20). The result would be shalom. He emphasized the fate of the wicked and in chapter 20 he accurately described their fate. He reiterated that God is in charge of His world and runs it His way. However, he misstated God's way and purposes.

These interpretations of God were at most "half-truths" and were not a blessing for Job because they misrepresented the Triune God and the cross, John 15:18-21, and Job's perspective of his relationship with God and God's with him. Zophar followed the pattern of Eliphaz and Bildad. All three failed to present the wholeness of God. God's tenderness — His love, mercy, and grace — was absent (20:1-29). Zophar believed that Job had sinned against him as well as against others and God (20:2). He is the least compassionate and most impatient of the three friends. Perhaps it was because Zophar spoke last and he had heard every speech and Job's responses.

Application

1. How does the phrase *listen to learn, to love, to lead* apply in any relationship?

2. When faced with a friend in trouble what is most appropriate for you to do?

3. After gathering the proper information, what is next most important for you to do?

4. What are some non-negotiable truths about God and man that are essential to properly interpreting any person's situation?

5. How are knowledge, trust, and faith linked?

CHAPTER 9

Job's Subsequent Responses: First Response

Job 6 and 7

JOB'S RESPONSES ARE RECORDED IN chapters 6-7, 9-10, 12-14, 16-17, 19, 21, 23-24, 26-31. His initial response was to Eliphaz as recorded in chapters 6-7. Job is distraught and acknowledged that his words were rash and impetuous as he appealed for sympathetic understanding (v.2-3). *The arrows of the Almighty are in me; my spirit drinks in their poison; God's terrors are marshaled against me* (6:4; see 7:14). Job knew that God was in control and therefore he was a marked man. That was not the issue. He did not like His control and himself as God's target! Job was in the throes of living the lie. His response is so common that it is expected and almost baptized by believer and unbeliever alike. A person may say that he or she is not Paul or Christ thereby shutting off any expectation of them to respond as Paul and Jesus did. Any response will do!

The response is in stark contrast to Christ's response to God and His providence — *not my will but yours be done* (Matthew

26:39; Luke 22:42; John 12:25-27). Pleasing and glorifying the Triune God means running and finishing the race well. These motivations drove Christ to the cross and beyond (John 4:31-34; 5:30; 6:38; Hebrews 12:1-3). They eventually drove Job and they are to motivate every believer.

You might say that Job was honest as he initially brayed against God and Eliphaz but paradoxically he wanted death in lieu of denying God (6:2-13, 8-10). Job claimed the right to bray and bellow via a series of rhetorical questions (6:5-10). He insisted that his words were justified. He still wished to die (6:8-9). He saw no light at the end of the tunnel; his hole was too deep and the mountain was too high for him to navigate himself out of his situation. Job was drowning in misery and in uncertainty. He demanded an explanation. In the midst of his once-in-a-lifetime experience Job had no answers. His theology had failed him. He thought his God was failing him! He considered himself lacking and he functioned as a person without resources and without hope (6:11-13; 1 Thessalonians 4:13; 1 Corinthians 10:13). He believed his circumstances confirmed his conclusions and that he was justified in expressing himself. However, as becomes evident in the book, Job came to agree that he had lived the lie. God had him right where he wanted him.

The two words, resource and hope, focus on control. They hold the key to victory in every situation because they point the believer to the God of circumstances, His resources,

and His hope. A proper vertical perspective is foundational
for hope God's way. It facilitates the believer's use of God's
resources, enabling grace and wisdom, for growth in Christlike
understanding, fear of the Lord, and joy (John 16:20-24; Romans
5:1-5; 8:24-25; 15:13; 2 Peter 1:10-11). Victory comes not necessarily
as the person is removed from the situation, but as the person
remains in it God's way for His glory (1 Corinthians 10:13). Hope
and resources are keys for every believer in every situation
(Romans 8:26-27; 2 Corinthians 1:3-4; 1 Corinthians 10:13; 1 Peter
1:13). God's resources are present but are not accessible with
physical eyes but through the eyes of saving faith and enabling
grace based on a proper understanding of God (2 Corinthians 5:7)

Job wanted spiritual help and from his brothers and now
(6:14-15). Job pondered the significance of his relationship with
God. Job wished for a divine suicide and that God would grant
him his wish — to crush him and cut him off. He wanted out
(6:11-13). He was in the abyss of doubt and confusion. After a
bit Job softened his tone and asked Eliphaz to make an honest
assessment of him (6:29-30). Interestingly, Job thought he had
made an honest interpretation of himself as did the three
friends who thought they had made an honest assessment of
Job! Everyone was wrong!

Chapter 7 contains a complaint against God (v.1-21). Job vividly
described and lamented his state of slave-like hard service (7:1-3,
4-6). He calls on God to remember the brevity of life (7:7-10).

In response he vows to cry out against this seeming injustice by God and compared his situation to the chaos caused by the "monster of the deep" (7:11-15). Job compared his situation to the primordial chaos as given in Genesis 1:2. Like the psalmist of Psalm 88, and I think sinfully, Job postulated that there was no hope, only darkness. Job, as was the psalmist, was in the midst of living the lie (see my website post in the third book of the Psalter, Psalm 88).

In 7:16-21, he expressed dismay and anger that he was under the unmerciful scrutiny of God who Job had considered was his friend. In that way, Job responded to God's providence as did David in Psalms 32 and 38 and the psalmist in Psalm 88. We are not told of the circumstances of Psalm 88. David's circumstances as recorded in Psalms 32 and 38 differed from those of Job. Job had no known specific sin to confess and David had failed to confess his sins. However, both men considered God's presence a burden. Job vacillated between God's presence as a burden and God's absence. Both agreed that God's presence needed to be "exorcised."

Job's mantra was and continued to be: *what was God up to* but he reasoned that if he was dead and in the afterlife, he would be able to remain true to God (19:25-27).Those words seem to express that Job desired a different classroom and setting for learning! Job's description of his condition was unrelenting unpleasantness and thus he believed he had the right to speak as he did (6:5-6, 10). If true, Jesus should have barraged the Father with questions and complaints!

Job described himself as willing to be a learner and having a desire to be taught. But he had *buts*. He considered himself resourceless, and thus hopeless (6:11-13). He was well into living the lie. He did not want to be accused without the facts being properly presented according to his scrutiny. He was concerned with what he believed was the undependability of his friends (6:14-15). Moreover, Job believed he had been targeted by God — *the arrows of the Almighty* (6:4; 7:14, 20-21; 16:12-13). Unknown to Job, this was a true statement. However, early on, Job missed God's purpose for His ways. I wonder what Job would have said to Christ!

Job pictured God as present but *actively silent*; Job proclaimed he would not be silent — he began a remonstrance about and against God and he expected God to "take it" (7:11, 17-20). Job did lament what he considered was the loss of communion with God (7:17-21). He spoke, but he assumed God was silent and perhaps worse still, not listening or listening and not caring. Sadly, these are common responses among Christians.

Job desired to have an audience with God in order to have God explain His actions. He did not desire fellowship with God. Job was moving down the slippery slope of idolatry and functionally reversing the Creator-creature distinction. God must give him what he wanted and deserved and the sooner the better! Interestingly, Job asked only for an explanation but not out of his situation. He thought relief would come when God answered him.

Job did not comprehend that his scenario was a mini-picture of Christ and the cross. Consider the comparisons: both left high positions, entered into hard times, and were betrayed by their friends. Job perceived himself as forsaken by God. Christ experienced what no believer will experience — separation from God as a result of the just Judge judging God's people in Christ. Unlike Job, Christ went to hell on the cross in order to please the Father and fulfill the eternal design of the Triune God (John 6:37-43).

Scripture records that the gospel was preached beforehand to Abraham (Galatians 3:8). We know that God provides every believer with everything he needs for life and godliness (2 Peter 1:3-4). We are not told of Job's understanding of the gospel. We do know that Job was a man after God's heart and in covenant with God (Job 1:1, 3; 8; 2:3). God takes care of His people and provides grace and knowledge. Job doubted those facts. He was living the lie.

Eventually and finally, victory did come to Job as a child of God, but it came in God's way and in His timing. As we shall read, Job was able to truly experience God (Job 38-42). God did not change. Victory in Christ required a change in Job. As a believer he was changed, and he discovered that he had much changing to do. Victory came as God was proved the King of Kings and Lord of lords. That fact may seem elusive in the "heat" of hard times, but it is sure and trustworthy because God is sure and trustworthy. The Cross and the Resurrection affirm those truths (Romans 4:25; 1 Corinthian 15:54-57). Later, Job took refuge, comfort, and joy in those simple but profound facts. However, in the heat of the battle, recalling and acting on the truth of who God is and what He is accomplishing, was not part of Job's "spiritual DNA."

As Paul recorded in 1 Corinthians 1:18-31, one of the lessons of the cross is rather simple: the way up and for understanding is the way down. Job had to experience and to cherish that simplicity. In his present situation, those truths were foreign to Job. The same was true for James and John as recorded in Matthew 20:20-28 and Mark 10:35-45. They sought the place of honor and glory. Although the circumstances differed, the principles were the same: God deserves to be honored and the way up to Him is the way down. Serving others is serving God. Such was the lesson of Christ who was the living ransom price paid out of love for and service to the Triune God.

How did Job get in this condition? I am not speaking of God's providence per se — those things that happened to him. I am speaking of Job's response to God and His providence. This man of God apparently had little experience with hard times. We don't know that for a fact, but there is no mention of previous hard situations in Job's life.

Moreover, man is a rational, emotive being; he thinks, and he desires. He responds based on his interpretative grid of biblical truth via saving faith *or* experience, reason divorced from biblical truth, and or feelings via purely relying on the senses such as eyes and ears. Often the person seems to be on the autopilot of feelings. Sadly, even in pleasant times, feelings and self tend to be a person's guide rather biblical truth.

In addition, man is patterned in his thought, desires, and actions. Thoughts and desire motivate actions or inactions which become habits. As an unbeliever, self has taken center stage in all these activities which flow from the whole person — inner and outer man. When a person becomes a believer, his motivation is toward pleasing God and away from pleasing self. However, there is remaining sinfulness in the believer which includes habituation for self, for and to sin, and for Satan (Romans 8:5-8, 9-11; Galatians 5:16-18). Old habits of thinking, wanting, and acting die slowly. The believer replaces self-pleasing in its various forms, including self protection with overriding desire to please the Father. In that way, he imitates Christ by using the circumstances to trust and obey his sovereign good God. Pleasing God requires the desire to please God; the knowledge of who God is and what He desires and deserves; the motivation to know and apply biblical truth;

and the energy and courage to die to self and live for God (Matthew 10:32-38; 16:24; Mark 8:34-38; Luke 9:23; 14:27; John 12:25). These terms describe the growing believer who simply trusts and obeys because God is good even when feelings and circumstances and perhaps others say differently.

All believers would do well to remember the words of Horatio Spafford's hymn: *It is Well with My Soul.* Faced with the loss of children and the near loss of his wife, he penned the words which have been a blessing to all believers throughout the ages. In one line in the hymn, he wrote that the Lord had *taught* him to say, it is well with his soul. I am not sure when and how he was taught. But Mr. Spafford was placed in God's classroom not as a punishment but as a blessing, personally and to others, now and then. What would Job's counselors have said to him! What would they have said to Christ?

Job would have done well to contemplate the truths expressed in the words of the hymn. All believers including Job must be engaged in looking at and through the circumstances at the God of them who is their God! Job needed help to do that, but his friends were more of a burden than a blessing. They did not provide comfort, compassion, or correction.

Application

1. How are Job's response in chapters 3 and 6 similar?
2. What is Job's goal?

3. What is Job hoping from his friends?

    a. Did he get it?

    b. Why and why not?

4. What is Job hoping from God?

    a. Did he get it?

    b. Eventually what did he get?

CHAPTER 10

Job's Subsequent Responses: Second and Third Responses

Job 9-10 and 12-14

JOB'S SECOND RESPONSE IS GIVEN in chapters 9-10. Job agreed with Bildad's conclusion as given in 8:20-22. Job, too, acknowledged that God doesn't reject a righteous man or strengthen the hands of an evil doer. He knows God will and has blessed him. God will fill Job's mouth with laughter and his lips with shouts of joy. But beginning in chapter 9, Job exclaims that these facts are what makes the present so distressing. He does not believe he is sinless but he wants a personal encounter with God — a day in court — to prove that he doesn't deserve this kind of providence (9:1-3, 14). At the same time Job acknowledged that God's wisdom and power are passed finding out (9:10). Yet he still wants answers his way and on his timetable.

God does not reject a blameless man but Job asked a forensic question: how can a man win an argument with God? *How can a man be righteous before God* (9:3)? Eliphaz had asked the same question (4:17). Job was aware of the Creator-creature distinction — he is not God. But he did not understand the significance of this truth in the moment. Therefore, Job demanded an explanation from God. As we shall see, increasingly, Job demanded that God give him an account (9:1-35). He increasingly questioned the righteous and goodness of God. He did not believe that he would get a hearing before God (9:16). Job did not get the hearing that he demanded and thought he deserved, but he received much more: God Himself! Job voiced his opinion that God was acting toward him randomly and purposelessly, without a game plan, and only as his enemy (9:17-18). Obviously Job did not know the whole story!

Chapters 9-10 are filled with courtroom terminology (9:3, 14-16, 24, 29, 32; 10:2, 17). Job wanted to know what charge God had against him (10:2). He accused God of being prosecutor, judge, and jury. Job concluded that his innocence and his relationship with God — was of no value. He wondered if he needed a mediator for his hoped-for courtroom appearance (9:33-35). He believed God took better care of the wicked — God despises the work of Job's hands and smiles on the wicked (10:3-7). These facts bring Job and all people face to face with the cross. Innocence does count. It was mandatory that Jesus be the innocent, holy, harmless, undefiled Lamb of God and the great High Priest (2 Corinthians 5:21; Heb. 4:15;

7:26; 9:14; 1 Peter 2:22; 1 John 3:5). Christ's innocence flowed from His deity, His virgin birth, and the indwelling Holy Spirit. It was one of the keys to His Messiahship and qualified Him as the true and perfect Messiah.

Job misunderstood himself, God, and the cross. Of note, in Job 9:4 and 14, Job acknowledged the reality of the power and justice of God but also his inability to comprehend it. This inability also points to the cross. Believers continue to marvel at the love of God as manifested by the Father Who judged the sinless Jesus as guilty and wrath-deserving in place of them. As he continued his discourses Job vacillated between trusting and unfaithfulness manifested by "on-God's-case."

Job's inability to rejoice in his God-given innocence which was in Christ was seen as a liability rather than a point of awe and reverence (Romans 3:21-26; 8:1). After his encounter with God, Job came to embrace confession and repentance as a gift and outgrowth of being in Christ (Job 42:6). I am sure he viewed the cross in a completely different way.

Job considered himself a man of sorrows (10:2-7). But that fact did not mean that Job had humbled himself. From Job's viewpoint (and David's as I have previously noted) God's sovereignty in the present situation was a burden (3:23-26; 6:4; 7:17-20; 10; 13:25-27; 14:16; 19:13-22; 30:16-19). Job, using human understanding as did Zophar, tried to fathom what his relationship with God meant for everyday life. At the same time, Job asked for his sin to be shown to him: 6:24; 7:20; 10:14-17; 19:4; 31:29-34. One might surmise that he wanted to repent in order to be restored thereby following the counsel of his three friends. I don't think that was it at all. Job wanted a guarantee of a restored fellowship with God for its own sake. He was not after things as Satan suggested. From the perspective of his circumstances, he believed he was out of fellowship with God or worse, God was out of fellowship with him. Job wanted to know how and why fellowship could be restored. Anyone sharing Job's thinking will have a misunderstanding and even a disdain for Christ and the cross.

Job continued to acknowledge God as Creator and Controller (Job 10:8-12). But Job's words convey the message that he did not like God's control. God was all-knowing, but Job believed that God refused to share His wisdom with Job and that He should (10:1-7). God created Job, and mankind, as His image bearer, but seemingly Job considered God uncaring who offered him no hope (10:8-17, 18-22). Those are strong words. I don't think Job demanded justice as much as he wanted and thought he deserved an explanation as to the why of God's sovereignty. As we shall see later Job tried to take God to court.

Job's third response is given in chapters 12-14. This is Job's second longest speech. Job perceived an unfathomable contradiction: a just and blameless man (God's terms for Job on three occasions) and yet he —Job — had received misfortune. Job began a litany of his problems and misfortunes (12:4-6). He was a victim of ridicule and a loser. In contrast, Christ was a winner in His humiliation because He humbled himself.

Victimhood seemed to be a favorite thought and theme running through Job's speeches. He pushed for an answer from God as to his condition. Yet at this time Job declared that God is sovereign in the created world and of history (12:13-25).

Not only did he consider himself a victim, but he also functioned as a demander and a would-be lawyer (13:1-3). Job still claimed God was his refuge: *though he slay me, yet I will hope in him* (13:15). What an amazing testimony especially in light of his previous statements. Job had vacillated between the idea of God who was non-hearing and uncaring but who was his God; between hope and hopeless, light and darkness, and victory and defeat. God had never let Job go. He had him right where He wanted Job. Job was barely holding on to God, but God held him firmly in His double grip (John 10:28-30). The vacillation was expressed in chapter 9: Job doubted that God would give him a hearing; in chapter 13: Job is convinced he will get a hearing and be vindicated; and in chapter 17: he is convinced only death awaits him.

God has every believer on a leash. The leash is different from the leash God has on Satan. God will never purchase and redeem His people and then lose them to their own ignorance and arrogance. As we shall see, Job repented of both (42:6). He humbly but joyfully and excitingly came to his senses (Luke 15:17-18). He could say with Solomon (paraphrase): don't talk so much, God is heaven, you are on earth, and let your words be few (Ecclesiastes 5:2-3). This godly counsel applied to both Job and the three friends.

Given his mindset, Job did not and could understand the cross and Christ's work as mediator. God knew Job needed a change in his thinking and wanting in order for Job to understand God and His work. Job expressed the thought that God's presence is everywhere, but it is a burden and he believes he is God's enemy (Job 3:26; 13:20-21, 34; 16:9; 23:2; 31:35; 33:7-11). Job wanted God to come out of hiding. The "bad guys" seemed to have it better than him (see Psalm 73 for a similar mindset and the solution and see my website regarding the Psalter and Psalm 73). Job professed his faith and his determination to trust God (13:13-15) . He knew that God rejects a godless man, but he was not that man (13:15: *though he slay me, yet I hope in him . . .* ; 13:20-21). Job was confident in his vindication (3:23-27). He perceived that his vindication in this life would be a sign that God's relationship with him and his with God was still solid. His vindication never came! Rather, a clear view of God and himself did and Job was overjoyed!

Application

1. God acknowledged what about God?
2. Words with forensic overtones abound in these chapters.
   a. Where was Job heading?

   b. What was he hoping to accomplish? Did it happen?
3. Job considered himself a victim and he perceived a contradiction: a just and righteous man inundated by calamity and misfortune.

   a. What was his answer?

   b. What would he demand from God?

CHAPTER 11

Job's Subsequent
Responses: Fourth, Fifth,
and Sixth Responses

Job 16-17, 19, and 21

JOB'S FOURTH RESPONSE IS RECORDED in chapters 16-17. Job held to his innocence and criticized his "miserable comforters" (16:2-5; also see 12:12; 13:1-12). Though innocent, he vowed to continue to suffer without understanding. As a physician I hear this response in various forms. People profess to be "sucker-uppers." Actually, they are proud people who live by the "I wants" and are often on God's case. Those words may seem strong but Job's description of himself in Job 42 helps put them in prospective (see my book: *Endurance: What It is and How It Looks in the Believer's Life).*

The phrase — to suffer — is an interesting one as I have pointed out previously. What in fact does it mean? Most people use the term to indicate an unpleasant and terrible experience and their response. The term refers to the milieu that the person has been placed by God whether occasioned by the person's own sin, being sinned against, or a combination. Job as do all believers faced the reality of God's control and providence. The term suffering is broader than the situation and experience itself. It refers to the person and his response in the situation, which is a response to God.

Again, in these chapters, Job painted himself the victim to and worn out in and by God's providence. Job pictures God as a ferocious lion out for a meal — him! (10:16; 16:7-9). This is a prelude for considering himself as targeted by God and His enemy (13:24; 16:9-14; 19:11; 30:24; 33:10). Job continued to describe his misery. He has supplied his own clothing — those of a mourner — who does not picture himself being vindicated by his friend (16:15-22). His only hope is a witness or advocate in heaven (16:18-21). It is interesting that he may be seeking the presence of God or at least someone in heaven who will be his advocate. Apparently, he thinks he will be welcome even though he has been on God's case!

According to Job, not only was God assailing him, but men were assailing him as well. Job was ready to check out — *my spirit is broken* (17:1). His victimhood was used as a reason to think and say what he did. He doubted that he would see the day of vindication in his lifetime (16:15-17:4). At this point, he simply wanted to function as a "sucker-upper." He had moved away from his initial desire of "divine suicide" (Job 3). He would simply tolerate and hang on (17:10-16). But for and to what was Job hanging in and hanging on? Job had no answer only demands. He believed he deserved an answer from God. He did not want to be on God's timetable. Rather the creature attempted to dictate to the Creator.

Job's fifth response is recorded in chapter 19 and included an appeal to God as his Redeemer (19:23-27, see the later section that addresses the possible theology of four passages including this one in regard to a mediator). Job was in distress in the midst of God's providence because of his view of God and the perceived lack of the vitality of his relationship with God. In 19:1-6, Job charged that God had wronged him. Both he and his friends, especially Bildad, believed and taught that God does not violate or pervert justice (8:3). Rather, all misfortunes and hard times are a tit-for-tat by and from God. They were deserved. In 19:7-12, Job described his view of God and asked where God was. He had received no answer to his cry (v.7). He concluded that God was silent because God was at war with him (19:8-12). Job would have had no answer for Jesus as He went to the cross.

Job added to his distress because of his perceived view of God and His active inactivity. In verses 13-19 of chapter 19, he stated that he was alone and lonely — everyone had deserted him. Jeremiah recorded this same experience (11:21, 23; 12:6). Jeremiah proclaimed the righteousness of God: *You are always righteous O Lord when I bring a case before you. Yet I would speak with you about your justice. Why does the way of the wicked prosper? Why do the faithless live at ease?* (12:1). The question or actually a demand or even an accusation is not unique to Jeremiah. Job addressed this issue in Job 21:7-15 as does Malachi (3:15). Both Jeremiah and Job wanted to know why the wicked prosper and they weren't! Psalm 73 highlights this request. Seemingly they played the victim card. They assumed circumstances and the presumed silence of God were testimony to their victimhood. Jeremiah had heard from God, but Job's God was silent, so he assumed. Job asked his friends why they were treating him as God was — without pity or care (19:21-22).

The seeming loss of fellowship with God greatly consumed Job. Please take note. In contrast to Satan's claim before God, fame, fortune, and fun did not motivate Job. Job focused on God's relationship with him. But that relationship did not seem to influence his response in his situation. Rather it was the perceived lack of its significance that influenced him. It was as if there was a one-way street — God to Job. Job demanded that God explain Himself, but Job himself was not required or motivated to give an accounting to God. He could think and say what he wanted about God!

Job was living the lie. God was alive and well. He was not silent or dead and He had not forsaken Job! (See Psalms 42-43 and Psalm 88 in the section under the Psalter on my website).

Circumstances cannot be a person's standard for assessing God and self. It was in this context that Job cried out for a deliverer. Perhaps he desired that the deliverer be God Himself (19:25-27 and see the section later in this book addressing four passages that refer to a mediator or go-between). The words may have proceeded from a conviction of saving faith (see Job 27:2).

Salvation and life after salvation are different sides of the same coin. Saving faith is a gift and necessary for salvation. Faithfulness in the use of the gift is to characterize the life of the believer after salvation. Job had not lost the gift of saving faith. God does not give gifts that are destroyed or lost. However, Job had not proven faithful in the midst of unpleasantness. This fact becomes clear in chapters 38-42. Early on Job would be a person who Christ characterized as you "O you of little faith" (Matthew 6:30; 8:26; 14:31; 16:8; 17:20). In the end, God answered Job's prayer and more! God gave Job Himself. But God did not give Job a reason for His providence. God expected, wanted, and deserved for Job, and all believers, to desire and enjoy God all the time. God uses various circumstances in order to accomplish His purposes.

Job's sixth response is given in chapter 21. In verse 4, Job continued to address his complaint to God and about God. In verse 22, Job gave a seminal statement: no one teaches knowledge to God. He is the One who teaches (35:11; 36:22; 38-41). Job's apparent high view of God was a defective view as was the view of God espoused by his three friends. Job's friends have referred to the fate of the wicked — God punished them (8:11-19; 15:20-35; 18:5-21; 20:20-25). Job insists on a different scenario as given in 21:7-15. These verses expressed the same view as did Jeremiah which I discussed earlier and as Asaph described in Psalm 73 verses 1, 5: *why do the wicked live on, growing old, and increasing in power.* Why do they prosper, and I am in trouble? Asaph, in the throes of God's hard providences, expressed a common theological standard in order to reevaluate his life as a Christian. He looked around at others and their circumstances — God's providence. He reasoned that perhaps he had made the wrong choice in believing in the sovereign Lord (Psalm 73:13-15). Similarly, Job asked, even demanded, to know why the wicked seem to win (also 21:7-15, 17-19). The wicked have no love or respect for God but only disdain. Job asked why God treats the wicked better than him? Ultimately Job was demanding "better" treatment from God than God gave His Son (21:23-32). Again, Job's theology, as was the three friends' theology, was opposed to the cross.

Job acknowledged God as all-knowing, but this all-knowing God must give Job an audience and give him an answer! In verses 27-33, Job knew the fate of the wicked and knew what his friends were saying: the wicked suffer, Job suffers, and therefore he is wicked. This logic was anything but a comfort to him. He thought they were being dishonest and wrong. God would agree (42:7-11). So would Jesus as He marched to and hung on the cross ministering all the while!

Application

1. Job has so much going on: agony, no explanation, friends who were not friends and a God who he believed had deserted him:

   a. How did he reach his conclusions?

   b. What was his basis?

   c. How did it "help" him if it did?

2. What will he learn in chapters 38-42?

3. What did Job need to do as given in Psalm 42:5, 11; 43:1; 73:16-19; Luke 15:17-18?

CHAPTER 12

Job's Subsequent Responses: Seventh and Eighth Responses

Job 23-24 and 26-31

JOB'S SEVENTH RESPONSE OCCURS IN chapters 23-24. In verses 1-7 of chapter 23, Job continued to proclaim his desire to have an audience with God. He complained to God but he did not know where to find God (v. 2-3). He still "felt" God's heavy hand and he desired a fair trial from the just Judge of the world. I wonder if Job knew that God would judge Christ, the sinless One, as guilty in his place (23:6-7; Genesis 18:25; 2 Corinthians 5:21), how he would have responded? Job had not convinced his friends regarding his innocence. Therefore, his only hope was to speak directly to God, but he was not convinced he would have that face-to face-meeting with God (23:8-10).

Job did repeat his commitment to being faithful (13:15; 23:3-4). But it was for redress and not praise and enjoyed intimacy with God. He believed he had been left in the dark (23:17). He began to think it was impossible to bring his cause before God for redress (23:3-9). He described God's presence as a heavy hand upon him (3:23; 23:2; 33:7-11). Apparently, never before had he experienced God's presence as a burden. He did not understand himself or God. The word translated *bitterness* and *bitter* in Job 7:11 and 23:2 (see also 3:20; 13:26; 10:1; 21:25; 27:2).is used fifteen times always with man as the subject and never God. The word describes an interpretation by man of God's actions or presumed inactions and resultant angst in one's heart or inner man as a result of God's providence. It is most commonly used in the book of Job and seems to picture the heaviness or discomfort and unpleasantness of God's presence. The words indicated a heaviness of David's soul — inner-man angst (see David in Psalms 32 and 38). Job perceived God as his Creator/Judge but not as his Father Who is carefully and tenderly watching over him.

Job acknowledged and described injustice in the world and equated it with God's presumed absence and silence in regard to him (23:1-12). Job does not believe he can find God no matter which direction he takes (23:8-10). Yet Job still sought an audience and a fair trial before God (23:6)! He had been fearful that he would not be able to speak the proper words before God, but now, for whatever reason, he believed he would be acquitted (9:14-20; 13:13-19; 23:6).

Job believed he stood alone but he still claimed monotheism (23:13). Again, the refrain: he is beside himself as to God's silence in his case and the lack of audience with Him. He has given up on God (23:15-16). God stands alone with no one to oppose Him especially Job! God carries out His decree against Job and as a result Job is faint-hearted; he has inner-man angst. Job is fearful but this fear of the Lord differs from that in Job 1:1:1; 2:3. This was sinful fear. Job believed he had no resources or hope and no God that cared. Job has intensified his attack on God. Yet in verses 21-24, Job seems to acknowledge that God is the just Judge but on His own timetable and Job was not on that timetable. Job wished for redress now for all "victims," especially himself.

Job's last and longest response is given in chapters 26-31. These chapters picture Job as one constantly vacillating between a pious, patient desire to hold on to God and the demand for God to explain himself. In chapter 26, Job extolled God's power and criticized the counsel of his unwise friends. It is ironic that Job extolled the greatness of God such that no man can understand Him: *Who then can understand the thunder of His power* (26:5-14). As previously stated, Job seemed to be impressed with God's wisdom and power and man's limited understanding of God, but these facts did not bring joy and comfort to Job nor did they change his approach to his situation and to God.

Job continued to wax and wane in his demands on God and in his trust in Him. Job proclaimed his faith in God by a solemn oath: *as surely as the Lord lives* (27:1-4). Job proclaimed that God had denied him justice and made him taste bitterness of soul. In spite of those facts, Job declares that he will not speak wickedness of God. In verses 5 and 6, he proclaims to the three friends that he is in covenant with God, and that he is innocent. Job seems to tout and focus on himself rather than on God.

He correctly described the ultimate fate of the wicked (27:13-23). These declarations are the fruit of saving faith — faithfulness to God and truth in thought, desire, and action. However, Job still considered himself a victim and he demanded God to give an account to him. He attempted to put God on his timetable by making demands on God. He functioned as if God owed him. These beliefs were in spite of the fact that he believed he had been denied justice up to that point (27:1). Yet, Job still continued to express faith in God's justice (27:7-10).

In the heat of God's providence, Job missed the joy of his salvation and the love of God (Jonah 2:10). You might ask: is that possible? Is it possible for anyone including Job to have the joy of his salvation given a burden such as Job's? The gospels and Jesus give a loud and clear answer: Yes! Jesus gloried in God and their relationship. The desire to bring glory to the Triune motivated Jesus to the cross and beyond. These are not simply pious and nice-sounding words. These are words to live by that express divine truth that Jesus knew and Job would learn. Truly the truth sets you free. It did Christ and it did Job.

Chapter 28 is the wisdom chapter. Job or the author of the book professed that fear of the Lord is wisdom and its source is God (28:20-28). Job knew but that knowledge per se was not a comfort. In chapter 29, Job described his former happy state (29:4); and in chapter 30, he contrasted it with his present condition and focused on his misery rather than God's purpose for him in it (30:27-31). As is true for all believers, Job did not know a specific purpose for God's providence. But as all believers know, Job was to honor God by continuing his patterned living which was characterized by shunning evil and loving God and his neighbor.

In general way, every moment of every day is the stage in which believers are to grow and change becoming like Christ in thought, desire, and action. The believer's patterned living — thinking, wanting, and doing — takes on more the character of Christ. Believers will trust when there is seeming darkness, will love when it seems impossible, and will obey when he or she wants to do their own thing. Circumstances may change how the above truths are expressed but circumstances don't change the validity and impetus to change and the believer's capacity to imitate Christ.

Chapter 31 contained Job's conclusion. He was devoted to maintaining his integrity. In verses 35-40, he finished his defense. He repeated the refrain that he hoped someone heard it (5:1; 9:33; 16:18-21; 19:25). In verse 35, he cried out to God: *let the*

Almighty answer me, which God began to do in Chapter 38. Job called for justice and Job got God!

Application

1. There is repetition in the book of Job. The book of Deuteronomy and 2 Peter are two books of the Bible that use repetition.

   a. What is the purpose for repetition?

   b. One purpose is for remembering (also see Psalms 105-106 for the beauty of remembering and the curse for forgetting).

   c. Remembering and forgetting involve both the inner and outer man: they focus on what?

2. Remembering and forgetting are both thinking activities. As a created, rational thinking being, a person will think God's thoughts or focus on a source of other thoughts — see 2 Corinthians 10:3-5.

   a. Psalm 119:9-11, 99-104: how do the psalmist's words minister to you and how do you apply these truths?

   b. What is the value of repetition and how does it relate to remembering and forgetting?

3. What is the repetition in the book of Job from the perspective of the three friends and from Job?

4. What is the purpose of repetition in the book of Job?

CHAPTER 13

Elihu, the Fourth Counselor

Job 32-37

NOT MUCH IS KNOWN ABOUT Elihu, the Buzite. Some have characterized him as a young gun out to show up the older generation and correct their errors. Others have pictured him as a prelude to God's interaction with Job. Either way, Elihu had flawed theology as well, but he was not rebuked by God. Moreover, he was concerned about the three friends and Job.

Zealous for helping, the younger Elihu apparently wanted to be a blessing. He patiently and respectfully waited for his opportunity to present himself and what he considered God's truth. He stepped onto the scene and presented his view of truth in four poetic speeches which served as an introduction to God's speeches (chapters 32-37: 32:6-33:33; 34:1-37; 35:1-16; 36:1-37:24). Elihu spoke and Job listened. Elihu was eager to share his knowledge (32:6, 10, 17).

Elihu was angry at the three friends (mentioned four times) because they had not dissuaded Job from his position. They were stalemated! Elihu attacked Job because he thought Job had presented himself more righteous than God (32:2: 27:5; 30:21). Elihu based his comments on his understanding of what Job had said. Perhaps that was one reason why God did not condemn him as He did the other three. Elihu was more than willing to let God refute and correct Job (32:13).

The opening of chapter 33 (v. 1-4) set the tone for Elihu's speeches and Job's meeting with God. Elihu challenged Job to be silent and listen which Job did! He was silent before God as well! He attempted to assume to speak as if God was speaking in response to Job's accusations. However, Elihu was wordy and protested too much about his own sincerity — *what I say is genuine and true*. As the others, he claimed to be upright. However, he was the only one who appealed to the Spirit of God who made him (Genesis 1:2; 2:7; Job 32:8; 33:4). Elihu seemed to know that wisdom comes only from the Lord and he believed he was God's agent. In contrast to Job, Elihu was sure God heard and answered Job (33:13-18). In verse 19, he introduced the concept that God uses hard times to prevent man from sinning (v.19; Romans 8:28-29; 2 Corinthians 4:1, 16-18; 12:7-10; Hebrews 12:3-4, 5-11). Paul expressed this truth in 2 Corinthians 12:7-10 (see my website post on this subject).

In chapter 34, Elihu defended God by reiterating truths about Him. He rebuked Job for accusing God of giving him what he does not deserve (34:6). He declared that God is not evil, unjust, partial, or unwise (34:10-20). Elihu made his concern for God's glory apparent (34:14-15). Elihu, as did the others, called for Job's repentance. Job was guilty and his angst and external circumstances proved it. The mindset of the four friends was "guilty until proven otherwise." Job's plight "proved" this assumed and reductionistic "fact." This thinking undermines the beauty of the Savior and the cross.

Follow the flow of Elihu's speeches. First, Elihu told Job he was not right. He accused Job of sin and rebellion (33:12-13). He asked Job why he was complaining to and about God since God is greater than man. Elihu was aware of the Creator-creature distinction. Elihu emphasized the importance of God's chastening, a point mentioned only once and that by Eliphaz, and a proper response to it (33:14-22; 5:17; Hebrews 12:5-12; James 1:2-4, 12; 1 Peter 1:6-7). He mentioned the possibility of redemption based on a mediator, a point mentioned only briefly by Eliphaz (33:23-28 and 5:1). I discuss this point later in the book. He emphasized Job's need to repent by highlighting God's gracious response to a sincere act of repentance (33:27-28).

Second, in chapter 34, Elihu bluntly accused Job of speaking without knowledge (34:34-37). God will agree with him (38:2). Ultimately Job agreed with both Elihu and God (42:3).

Third, as did the others, Elihu referred to Job's problems as stupidity, lack of insight and rebellion. His charges were based on his view that Job spoke without knowledge and lack of insight and that he acted like a wicked man (34:35-36; 35:16). Interestingly, as did Elihu, God rebuked Job for speaking without knowledge (38;2-4; 40:3). Moreover, Job accused his friends of speaking without knowledge thereby offering him no comfort (12:3, 9; 13:1-12, 16:2-5). In chapter 42, God would agree (v. 7-9). A logical conclusion follows: only God and those who are properly related to Him speak truth. Therefore, only truth sets the believer free.

Fourth, Elihu agrees with the friends. He, too, has limited theology. He sees no way out of the dilemma for Job other than to have him repent. Yet, the call to repentance is a type of moralism similar to the counsel given previously by the three friends and for the purpose of getting. The four counselors seemed to agree with Satan's prediction to God. Satan had predicted that since Job only wanted something from God, Job would "fold" under pressure. Satan purposed that God was more than willing to placate Job and all His creatures simply to "look good." Repentance was a way to get rather than to glorify God and if done for that reason, Job would have followed Satan's prediction. Satan charged and attacked God as a potential loser, a user, and a buyer of people for His own gain. In other words, God wasn't worthy of worship, praise, and love.

All five of the players (Job and the four counselors) spoke of justice and comfort but none spoke of God's love, mercy, and grace. All four missed the fact that Job seemed to truly miss and long for fellowship with God. Moreover, they failed to realize that Job wanted to be assured that his relationship with God and God's with him was intact and properly functioning. They missed the wisdom of the cross. You can only wonder what they would have told Jesus.

In chapter 36, Elihu boasted of perfect knowledge — either the possessor of it or the communicator of it (36:4). In 37:16, he applied the phrase to God. Elihu offered truths that he thought had been hidden or not covered. He reiterated fundamental truths about God: God is mighty and just. Therefore, His purposes will be fulfilled (v. 5-7). Verses 6-9 are classical statements of God's justice in rewarding the righteous and punishing sinners. In verses 8-10, Elihu called attention to God's intention for unpleasant times. God uses "hard providences" to get man's attention (30:11; 36:6, 8-10, 21). In the context of hard times, God exposes sin. God intends to test and train His people in and by them. However, Elihu's words remind me of the fatigue and effort expended in military combat simply out of duty. Love for and devotion to the Commander and the anticipation of hearing the refrain of thankfulness for a job well done were missing. Elihu's words tend to have a hard, harsh, grinding, and biting character.

Yet Elihu encouraged Job: *God is wooing you Job, so don't blow it* (my paraphrase of 36:16). However, Elihu missed an important point. With tender compassion and covenantal faithfulness, God brings His people back to Himself (Hosea 2:14-15, 16-17, 18). God is the Covenantmaking and Covenantkeeping God, who is

His people's Father and their Husband (Exodus 4:22-24; Hosea 2:16-17; Jeremiah 3:4, 19; 31:9, 32).

All the counselors missed an important truth. God grows His people and He does so in all types of situations. Both hard and easy times are God's providence and must be viewed from that perspective (Proverbs 30:7-9). The writer of Proverbs did not want too much poverty or too many riches. Each has its own trouble (Matthew 6:34). Moreover, both are to be used to become more like Christ. The book of Job concentrated on hard times and the proper response to them based on a proper perspective of God, self, others, and providence.

Elihu did present truth about God and His ways (Romans 5:1-5; James 1:2-4; 1 Peter 1:6-7). But all the counselors missed the point that all of God's providence are to be viewed as coming from God sovereign, good hand and are to be used to glorify God by becoming more like Christ (Romans 8:28-29). I repeat: neither riches nor poverty necessarily point to God's favor or curse. Using hard times to grow and change thereby honoring God is counterintuitive and counter-cultural. However, when the believer, in any situation (every situation is God's providence), calls to mind and applies biblical truth, life is simplified, and God is glorified. God delivers His people, not from the situation necessarily, but in the situation, as they think, desire, and act in a God-pleasing manner (1 Corinthians 10:13). Becoming more like Christ is the only way to truly glorify God because Christ is the glory of God who explains the Father, and it is in Christ that we see God (2 Corinthians 4:4, 6; John 1:18; 6:46; 14:6-9).

Job and the four friends shared the same theology. They considered hard times as a sign of God's displeasure. Therefore, they missed the true meaning of the cross. Job interpreted his experiences as loss of an intimate relationship with God. The friends interpreted hard times as God's discipline. By inference, the absence of hard times — easy times — were interpreted as God's favor. This approach to God and His providence would never explain the cross. Based on their theology, Jesus was a loser. Their counsel to Jesus would have been to repent! Every person who has had hard times must be a loser as well, but repentance will restore them.

In verses 17-21, Elihu continued to offer hope to Job but his evaluation of Job differed from that of God's (36:21 compared to 1:8 and 2:3). That hope is summarized as: don't simply embrace God's providence whatever it may be (v. 20-21). Rather, redeem the time (Ephesians 5:15-18). While a good start, none of the counselors spelled out this truth, its motivation, or how it should look in Job's life. Their answer was simply to repent in hopes of *reversing* rather than *redeeming* the times. In the end, Job came to taste God for who He is and not what He gives. His focus was on the relationship with God, its reality, beauty, and satisfaction. That is heavy but divine and sweet theology (Genesis 50: 19-21; Psalm 34:8; Romans 8:28-29).

In anticipation of God's speeches in Job 38-41, Elihu at the end of chapter 36 and in the first thirteen verses of chapter 37 described God's awesome power in nature (36:27-37:13). In verses 14-18 he challenged Job to *stop and consider God's wonders.* He challenged Job to ponder God's power as Job considered and answered a series of questions: did he know how God controls the clouds and hangs them (v. 15-16)? Could he join God in spreading out the skies (v. 18)?

In verses 19-24, Elihu prepared Job for God's coming. In verse 19, he put Job on the spot: *Tell us what we should say to God?* In verse 22, he concluded: No one should demand an audience with God because God is holy — *God comes in awesome majesty* (Psalm 48:2; Isaiah 6:1-10). Because God is God — holy and beyond mankind — God is to be feared. Elihu concludes: Therefore, *men revere him* (v. 24). Yet Elihu presented only one side of a multisided coin. Interestingly, Job did fear the Lord (1:1, 8; 2:3) but Job had not grown in the understanding of Who God is and how He worked! Fear of the Lord is the foundation of wisdom and it moves people to God not away from Him (Proverbs 1:7). It enables God's people to rest in God and to understand and understanding strengthens faith and faith strengthens understanding. Job was about to face the living and real God. In essence, Elihu told Job to get ready for the experience of his life. And it was!

Application

1. Elihu takes on Job in ways the three friends did not.

   a. How was he different?

   b. How was he the same?

2. Elihu wooed Job by pointing to God's power and justice rather than His mercy. God's right as the just Judge of all the earth had collided with Job's presumed right to know. How will God resolve this seeming dilemma?

3. Elihu pleads with Job for patience (36:1ff). However, the answer to Job's problem is not to be found in God's justice only. Rather in response to both God's power and goodness, Job must trust and obey.

   a. What was Job missing?

   b. What was Elihu missing?

   c. What were the three friends missing?

4. Job and his friends were looking for reasons for Job's condition. Yet they knew God was in control. Elihu encouraged Job to look up to God Himself in order to find the purpose and goal of God's providence.

   a. What did it take for Job to do that?

   b. What will it take for you to do that?

   c. What did Job discover and what have you discovered?

CHAPTER 14

God's Meeting with Job: Part I

Job 38-42

THE LAST CHAPTERS OF JOB (38-42) record God's two discourses with Job (38:1-40:2; 40:6-41:34). God orchestrated the meeting. God was always in control. To see God's face (to be in His presence) was believed to bring death (Genesis 16:13; 32:30; Exodus 24:10; 33:20, 23; Leviticus 10:1-4, 10-11; Numbers 12:8; Judges 6:22; 13:22; Isaiah 6:5). Yet, amazingly Job sought to see God and in God's presence Job did not die. This Old Testament teaching probably influenced the nation of Israel and their view of Jesus. They rejected Him and refused to acknowledge Jesus as God, let alone Lord in part because He looked like any other Jew and they were in His presence and they did not die (John 1:6-11). The Israelites saw and some even touched and were touched by Jesus. Moreover, they knew His origin and His parents, so they thought! They were sure Jesus was not God.

Phillip, perhaps hoping for a theophany, told Jesus to show (demonstrate) them the Father. He, like the Pharisees, wanted a sign (Matthew 12:38-42; 16:1-4)! The request seemed logical to

the disciples because even though God Incarnate was standing
before them; they had not died (John 14:6-9). They had physical
eyes and ears, but their spiritual senses were still defective.
Jesus came to set His people free (Luke 4:18-22). The disciples
and the people asked: could Jesus really be God, let alone the
Redeemer of Israel? Philip was unsure but Israel's answer was
deafening and a rebellious "no." The people and the disciples
had seen and heard Jesus — had a sensual experience — but
they did not know Jesus. The disciples had not come to know
Jesus as much as they loved Him. Their love was defective
because it was, in part, based on a lack of understanding of
who Christ was and who they were (see John 13:1-2). Such was
the case with Job. As the disciples would, Job came to know
God intimately (Philippians 3:7-11).

At last Job was getting what he wanted — a personal
encounter with God. He had no inkling that this encounter
would be the means of a great change in him. Job had charged
God with wrongdoing although he knew that God was in
control. That knowledge made God and his situation all the
more confusing and enigmatic (9:3; 10:3; 12:4-6; 16:11; 24:1-12;
21:16; 22:18; 27:2). Ironically as we have discussed, Job's faith in
God continued. He continued to hang on to God but wondered
why and for how long. This is a testimony to God as much as
it is to Job (John 10:28-30)! According to Job the fact that God
had made a mistake seemed to be the only explanation for Job's

predicament. The conclusion was based on Job's reasoning: the Judge was blindfolded (9:24). Job claimed that God could not see but was apparently satisfied.

In these last chapters (38-42) the author uses God's covenant name: I AM. I AM spoke from the whirlwind or storm which is a picture of the chaos of Job's life (38:4; 40:6). Elihu had anticipated the appearance of the divine presence in full splendor and majesty from which Job would hear God's voice (37:22). Job had previously acknowledged that God was all-knowing and the Revealer (9:4; 12:13, 22; 28:12, 20, 23). He demanded that God reveal His reasons for his situation which God never did. Job had taken issue with God's governing activity but now Job was in the presence of God!

God addressed Job's accusations against the darkness of God's control in a remarkable manner. He challenged Job with questions that addressed His Being and His activity (38:3, 12-13, 22). God introduced the subject of the Creator-creature distinction. God's questions pointed to the reality of the Creator, His creation, Job, and God's providence. They pointed to the "bigness" of God (Lord of lords and King of kings, Creator and Controller) and the "smallness" of Job (the creature and image bearer of God).

God presented truth and ignored Job's situation (I am indebted to Dr. Stephen Davey's sermon/lecture series on the book of Job: Wisdom for the Heart — wisdomonline.org).

God asked Job a series of questions based on Job's thought about who God was and how He ran His world. God presented evidence to Job's senses — the physical eye and ear — that was interpreted in both Job's heart (inner man) and his brain according to a standard. Remember man is a whole person — inner and outer man! As does everyone, Job was to interpret the facts either God's way or his way. God's premise was this: to date Job had wrongly interpreted the facts that he had taken in by his senses. God was giving Job insight into Himself and His power, control, justice, and goodness to enable Job to get victory no matter the circumstances.

Initially and functionally, Job had returned to the Garden of Eden and followed in Satan's footsteps. According to satanic logic, God owed Job, and all mankind, reasons for how He runs His world. Satan opposes God's control but he is in competition with God. He is the loser! God does not bless His competition (Isaiah 42:8; 48:8-11)!

You might wonder what made the questions so tough for Job to answer. It boils down to the simple, everlasting truth: God is God and Job is not. God was getting ready to reverse Job's sinful misunderstanding and misuse of the Creator-creature distinction. God set the record straight which is a preview of the cross (Romans 3:21-26). God will always be God and Job the creature. Everyone is to be in their proper place. God created chaos and from chaos He created the cosmos and order

(Genesis 1:2: *the earth was formless, void, and dark.*). God gave the cosmos order and design by separating and gathering on days 1-3 and by making and filling on days 4-6.

Post-fall, order and chaos occur together. Chaos, darkness and spiritual deadness are the result of Adam's sin and God's judgment. God did not intend for Job or mankind to desire a return to chaos and darkness which he demanded in Job 3. Order is God's good gift to His creation and pictures redemption. Evil and grace co-exist in God's post-sin world. The world awaited God's life-giving and order-making creation which comes fully in Jesus Christ. His coming sets the stage for re-creation — redemption. Creation and re-creation are linked. Jesus and God are light (John 8:12; 9:5; 12:46; 1 John 1:5). Jesus stepped into darkness and mingled with those in darkness who loved the darkness (John 3:17-21, 36). He was bringing a new creation and a new mode of existence.

Job and his friends had missed these profound truths partly out of ignorance and partly out of arrogance. Therefore, they had misrepresented the cross and the God of the cross. They missed the function of God's providence and the beauty of becoming more like Christ with whatever providence God provides. As a result, Job was burdened and not blessed.

In these chapters, God pointed Job to His power and wisdom as manifested in nature in contrast to Job's impotence. It was as if the author of the book of Job knew Romans 1:18-23. God asked Job where he was when God created the heavens and the earth (38:4-5; see Proverbs 30:4 and Romans 11:33-35). All nature sings and rings the presence, power, wisdom, and beauty of God (Psalm 24:1-2).

In chapter 38:4-38, God presented inanimate creation as a testifier of His sovereign power and control: the earth (38:4-7, 18), the sea (38:8-11, 16), the sky (38:12-15), and the weather (38:22-30). God pointed to its complexity and beauty. God asked Job to ponder the fact that He did not ask any human regarding creation or divine purpose (38:4-7). Job played no role in creation let alone being present when God spoke and it was so. God asked Job for his opinion and insight (38:18) regarding light and darkness (38:19-20), water (38:22-23), and the stars (38:31-33). God both restrains and protects that which may be hostile to human existence. These facts do not deny the reality of God's hard providence — tough times — for believer and unbeliever. God had Job focus on who he was against the backdrop of God's handiwork — creation. Job was wisely silent throughout both discourses apparently humbling himself.

David, in Psalm 8, also pictured man in the backdrop of the Creator and His handiwork, creation. David marveled at the position God had placed man. David penned these truths while on the run from enemies within and without Israel and his family. His position — God's providence — was similar to Job's. David, God's agent to build a kingdom of righteousness and peace, was humbly amazed that God was even mindful of man.

David viewed the Creator and His creation, the heavens and the earth, and developed a radical view of mankind's position in God's world. It was as if David, and ultimately Job, understood the absurdity of Creator-denying satanic-engendered falsehoods such as evolution.

In chapters 38:39-39:40, God moved to animate creation. You might say that God took Job to the zoo. From a human perspective these animals are mysterious, and their milieu creates "natural paradoxes." God brought to Job's thinking a number of animals with differing characteristics: a strong animal, the lion (38:39); a restless, jumpy animal, the raven (38:41); a fearful animal, the mountain goat (39:1-2); a stubborn animal, the wild donkey (39:5-8); a robust and durable animal, the wild fox (39:9-12), an odd animal, the ostrich whose eye is bigger than its brain (39:13-18); the courageous, royal animal, the horse (39:19-25), and lastly, the amazing hawk who depends on amazing eyesight (39:26-30). All of these are endowed by God to function and survive. At the conclusion of God's opening speech, Job must have recalled his words in 31:35: *Oh that I had someone to hear me! I sign my defense — let the Almighty answer* (5:1; 9:33; 16:18-21; 19:25). How quickly Job would come to his "senses." He grew in his faithfulness and understanding via an inside out change in his thinking about himself, God, and God's providence. This change occurred when he was confronted by the living God and His creation. Such it should be for all of God's children.

At the end of the first discourse, Job answered God (40:3-5). He said he was unworthy and he will not speak. The word translated unworthy occurs about 80 times and carries the idea of being slight, lowered, and even being cursed. He had said enough. Many in Scripture have come to this same conclusion when confronted with the presence, power, and performance of God. The nearer one draws to God, the more he is able to acknowledge and confront his own unworthiness and the more he guards his tongue and his heart (Genesis 18:25; Isaiah 6:5; Ezekiel 1:28; Matthew 3:11; 8:8; Luke 5:8; 7:6-8; John 1:27; 3:30).

God did not stop His loving cross-examination of Job. He moved to the Behemoth (40:15-24) and the Leviathan (41:1-34). No one is sure what kind of animal was the Behemoth. It was a great, massive beast. Yet God created and controlled it. The description of the Leviathan is the longest, most detailed description of an animal in the Bible. Many theories have been put forth regarding this animal. Suffice it to say that God made His point: God is the Creator and Controller and is worthy to be trusted. A mere man can't instruct God. It was not his original design and only serves to complicate life by dishonoring God.

The apparent absence or at least the silence of God and Job's perceived view of God as impotent and apathetic were major issues for Job. But there was another major issue for Job: entitlement. Job believed that God was using His power incorrectly. He thought he deserved an answer from God. Job had concluded that God had deserted him. Job's feelings and circumstances told him so. He interpreted his circumstances through the grid of what he considered was God's silence and or absence. Based on his theology, Job would have misinterpreted the three hours when darkness came over the land as Jesus hung on the cross and underwent the full fury of the wrath and justice of God (Matthew 27:45-47; Mark 15:33-34; Luke 23:44-45).

One of God's purposes in presenting the creation and His creative activity centered on the Creator-creature distinction. God confronted Job with His greatness as a means of acknowledging and appreciating the great divide between God and mankind. Only then would man acknowledge and humble himself before the cross. If there is no divide, there is no need of the cross and a divine Savior. All is one — pantheism. As recorded in Isaiah 6:1-10, God chose to put His glory and holiness on display. Isaiah got the point: he humbled and prostrated himself thereby making himself ready for service. In John 12:41, John wrote that Isaiah saw God's glory in his vision of the pre-incarnate Christ. Isaiah spoke of the glory of God (Isaiah 6:3) and John spoke of the glory of Christ. He made no distinction. Christ is the glory of God. When you have seen Christ, you have seen the Father — they are One (John 14:6-9; 10:30; 17:24-26). If the distance behind God and man, especially post-fall, was to be bridged, God would have to be the Builder of that bridge. He did in Christ by the Holy Spirit (John 1:47-51 and Genesis 28:12).

God was intent for Job to be the man who was blameless and upright, a man who modeled Christ. That is His creational design for all believers and the Church (Ephesians 1:4; 5:27). Only then would Job imitate Christ, as would any believer, by trust and obedience. Only then would God be glorified and exalted. These activities are to be motivated not simply by duty but more: from privilege and blessing (1 John 5:3-4). Every believer including Job should not misinterpret circumstances. The believer is not to interpret God through circumstances; he is to begin with God and His Word. Accordingly, he will interpret circumstances based on God's presence, promises, power, provisions, plan, and purposes. As a result, Job and every believer will grow because they are thinking God's thoughts, desiring what God desires, and acting accordingly. In a nutshell, God saved Job and all believers to imitate Christ. In that way Christ is fully glorified. When Christ is glorified, the Triune God is glorified which is a foretaste of heaven (John 17:24-26)!

In these last chapters, as I have mentioned, God never addressed His providence and Job's unpleasantness and the reasons for it. God had other items on His agenda! He didn't vindicate or condemn Job even though Job said he wanted to be vindicated. God did rebuke Job and pushed His agenda. Job finally got it! God is patient and long-suffering, covenantally faithful from beginning to end. Circumstances, experience, human reasoning alone, and feelings don't change the truth of God and His loving control.

God concludes His first speech with the words recorded in chapter 40:1-2: *the Lord said to Job: Will the one who contends with the Almighty correct him? Let him who accuses God answer him.* So far Job had been closed mouth. What else could he do? God repeated a challenge to Job. Job's request was answered, and God had spoken to him personally. What does Job have to say now? God's question was as much as a challenge as it was a rebuke. Having armed Job with true knowledge, God invited a response from him. In addition, God brought a charge against Job (40:2). Job had accused God of wrongdoing and required Him to give an explanation for His actions. In spite of those facts, God spoke directly to Job. It was out of His relationship with Job that God spoke. This fact alone proves that Job was never alone. Times were tough but God had not left or forsaken him (Genesis 15:1-3; Deuteronomy 31:6, 8; Joshua 1:5; Hebrews 13:5-6). Job had lived the lie. A major reality for all believers was introduced at this point: if Job, one of God's best, did not get the awesome nature and beauty of God and His work and its impact on Job, who would? Christ proved to be the true man of God who got it.

Job began to get it as given in 40:3-5: *Then Job answered the Lord, "I am unworthy — how can I reply to you? I put my hand over my mouth. I spoke once but I have no answer — twice but I will say*

no more. Job's unworthiness referred to his recognition that
he was a *lightweight* (see Luke 15:17-18). He had no reputation
or heaviness when he considered himself next to God. He was
not even on the same playing field! God is the real heavyweight,
a Being of maximum and supreme majesty and reputation.
Those words are so easily jettisoned especially during hard
providences. Job was in the process of humbling himself. He
was making a correct assessment of himself with God as His
standard. But notice that Job does not repent. He was not there
yet. Out of love and mercy and a real jealousy for His name,
God pressed on as shown in the last chapters.

Chapter 42 is the grand finale. In it Job makes a massive
testimony about himself and God. He accentuated the Creator-
creature distinction. Moreover, he embraced it as good, holy, and
of great benefit. Job was now seeing God through the eyes of
saving and sanctifying grace. His interpretive grid had changed.
Job was saved, but he had not fully trusted in God (Proverbs
3:5-8). He trusted himself but he still hung to God's truth about
God. Job's statement in chapter 42 (v. 1-4) emphasized the initial
activity of his physical eyes. His interpretive grid had been the
physical, the material, and the *now* through and by the senses.
He had lived sensually. He had seen with physical eyes and
heard with physical ears but without the interpretive grid of
biblical truth. Job had biblical truth, but it was incomplete and
defective. Therefore, he did not properly perceive God and His

ways. As a result, he was drowning in his feelings. He had little hope; darkness was his friend (3:1-26). As a result, he lashed out at God and his friends. Interestingly, he never rebuked God for giving him his three friends.

Now Job had a heart change and with it, his thoughts and desires changed. Job was already saved but he had not acted as a child of the King. He had been living the lie! Now he desired growth. He acknowledged that his spiritual and heart blindness had been removed. His interpretative grid had been replaced. He had been in darkness but now he is in the light as he is light (Ephesians 5:8-14). Job was functioning suprasensuality — by saving and sanctifying grace and faith — rather than by his mere senses (2 Corinthians 5:7).

Let's tread softly here. Job was not like the religious teachers of Israel and most of the Israelites of Jesus' days. Those people rejected the true light because they loved darkness (John 1:4-5, 10-11; 3:19-21, 36). Job loved the Light. Yet by his own words he functioned in darkness. In his own words he said that he was unwise and more in the dark than he realized. He had lived the lie. Now what he saw with the physical eyes, he rightly interpreted with a changed heart — his inner man. What he saw now he saw with the eyes of saving faith — his spiritual eyes and his interpretation was correct and honored God (John 7:24; 8:15; 1 Corinthians 13:12; 2 Corinthians 5:7; 10:7). Moreover life was simplified!

Application

1. Chapters 38-42 are remarkable passages that bring together many truths about God, the world, and man. Begin to make a list of those truths.

2. Job was a special man who had a special place in redemptive history. How does his story point to and help you understand the cross?

3. How does Job's story help you understand relationships?

4. How do you view God's seeming silence? See Psalms 32, 38, and 73; Luke 15:17-18.

CHAPTER 15

God's Meeting with Job: Part II

THE OPENING VERSES OF CHAPTERS 40 and 42 are critical for understanding the book of Job. Job is God's man picked from eternity past as an instrument to present the truth to the world that God is God and man is not. Acting on that simple yet profound truth would have prevented Adam from acknowledging and acting upon satanic-derived counsel. Satan began in the Garden by casting doubt on God's previous counsel (Genesis 2:15-17). He attacked God's goodness and truthfulness (Genesis 3:1-5). Any attack on God's counsel is an attack on God.

In the book that bears his name, Job is presented as a man who is in covenant with God. He is God's man, a man of integrity, blameless and upright. He knew that God was relational and that his own relationship with God was of upmost importance. However, in God's providence, Job was thrust into the middle of extreme unpleasantness. What would Job do? He had to rely on biblical truth or information from some other source as his interpretative grid. Job and his friends confirmed that every fact must be and is interpreted through some grid.

Job's circumstances were initially interpreted by his three friends as an indication that Job was out of proper relationship and favor with God. They used feelings, experience and mysticism, tradition, and knowledge divorced from biblical truth as their standard. Job appealed to his understanding of God and His ways — God as he knew Him. Given his circumstances, he concluded that God had it wrong. His view of his relationship with God and God with him convinced him that his friends were wrong. He did not want to believe that his circumstances pointed to a defect in his relationship with God and that repentance was the answer. His friends' counsel only aggravated the situation. Initially from the "darkness of his soul," he appealed to God. Yet, he believed God had not and would not answer him. Thus, he demanded an audience — an in-your-face time — with God.

Job received much counsel from his friends. Their reasoning was one-sided, reductionistic, emphasized God's justice and retribution, and repentance as a tool to gain God's acceptance and favor. Their counsel only intensified Job's inner-man angst. Job discarded the friends' counsel and replaced it with his own. His conclusion was not an improvement on his three friends' counsel. He concluded that God had made a mistake. He perceived God's presence and control as a burden. At the same time, he held to the belief that God was in control, but he interpreted God's providence as evidence of God's absence or apathy. He considered God only as a silent bystander. In fact, Job functioned for a short time as a deist. In the end he acknowledged that he was the real problem.

Job was changed as a result of his encounter with the living God. His understanding of God, self, and man was expanded. His understanding of reality and the dynamics of God's providential control changed. Job had to change his thoughts and desires about God and himself. He acknowledged that he must decrease and God must increase (Luke 5:8; John 1:27; 3:30). Job's repentance and intercession for his friends indicated that he had humbled himself.

God asked: *Will he who contends with the Almighty correct him? Let him who accuses God answer him (Job 40:2).* Each word in the passage *(contend, correct,* and *accuse)* carried judicial overtones (also see Job 9:16-20, 22-24, 29-35; 10:1-7, 13-17, 13:3, 6, 24; 16:9, 21; 19:1-6; 31:35; 33:10-13, 35-37). Initially Job was concerned about God's charges against him; he wanted to defend and vindicate himself even if he required an advocate (13:3, 6, 15; 16:19-21). However, as his condition continued and his three friends were no help but a hindrance, Job thought it necessary and proper for him to take the just Judge of all the earth to court and have Him answer to him (Genesis 18:25; Acts 17:24-28). Job attempted to reverse the Creator-creature distinction. Job told God that He needed a lawyer!

Job first answered God by confessing that he was unworthy (of no weight, not even a light weight) when he stood before

God the Heavyweight (Job 40:4-5). Job spoke from the heart that he was the fool. He had opened his mouth too many times! His three friends accused him of this very thing and of being wise in his own eyes (8:1-3; 11:2; 15:1-6; 18:2; 20:4-5; Proverbs 3:5-8). Now in God's presence, Job chose not to speak. Job was truly growing in wisdom! But Job did not repent.

God questioned Job regarding mankind's impotence in restraining wickedness and saving itself (40:9-14). Man can't even restrain the behemoth, the land monster (40:15-24) and Leviathan, the sea monster (41:33). In chapters 40:7-41:34, God continued the description of the most powerful land and sea creatures in two poems (40:15-24; 41:1-11). Both the behemoth and the Leviathan are God's creatures.

The first ten verses of chapter 41 were aimed at convincing Job how helpless he was in the presence of such frightening creatures, let alone in the presence of his Creator. These verses and Job 40:24 (*Can anyone capture him by the eyes or trap him and capture him by the nose*) make similar points: they emphasized the folly of interacting with the leviathan and the behemoth. Verse 11 of chapter 41 posited a ground-breaking truth when God asked Job: *Who has a claim against me that I must pay? Everything under heaven belongs to me.* Wow! God stated His ownership in no uncertain terms: I own everything including you, Job (Psalm 24:1-2; 50:7-12). In essence, God asked Job: Who do you think you are?

God provided the longest poem centered on the most terrifying creatures as a fitting climax to His personal encounter with Job (41:12-34). In verse 12, God argued from the lesser to the greater. It is folly and arrogance to stir up God's great and awesome creatures. It is a greater folly and arrogance to oppose God. If these creatures spark dread due to their awesomeness, how much more should their Maker and Controller. Opposing either makes no sense. God warned Job, and us, against arrogance and irreverence (which is breaking the third commandment). God emphasized the Creator-creature distinction.

God's purpose in highlighting His sovereignty was proactive and not reactive. God did not intend to shut up Job and discourage him from interacting with Him. Rather, God highlighted and demonstrated His right and might to run His world His way for His glory and the good of His people. God intended this truth to be a blessing and comfort as did Jesus who taught that He was truth and the Truth sets a person free (John 14:6; 8:31-32).

Job continued his testimony in Job 42:2-3: *I know that you can do all things; no plan of yours can be thwarted. Surely I spoke about things that I did not understand, things too wonderful for me to know.* Job quotes God's words as given in Job 38:2-3 and 40:7. Job agrees with God — this is confession. Job gave a verdict of himself: he had spoken as if was a wise person. He had the wrong standard. Compared to God and His truth, he was ignorant. He acknowledged that God's knowledge and his knowledge were not on the same playing field. God is God and he is not. He assumed God owed him. He was wrong.

Job rejoiced in the newfound truth that God owes him nothing, but at the same time, he understood that God had given Himself to Job and the personal meeting testified to that fact. Job continued in verses 5-6: *You said, Listen now and I will speak. I will question you and you will answer me. My ears have heard of you but now my eyes have seen. Therefore I despise myself and repent in dust and ashes.* This is the cry of a humble, liberated man. The cry meant that Job had learned that God was a far greater Being than Job had imagined and that he was much smaller than he had acknowledged. Job had had a high view of himself, a low view of God, and functioned accordingly. He had demanded that God give him an accounting.

By grace, Job heard and responded as a true child of God. Job now knew that evil and trouble are part of God's plan and His providence. With this knowledge, Job could understand the cross correctly. This new understanding forced him to the Garden and to revisit Adam and Eve and their choice: they chose Satan and self over pleasing God. Satan will never acknowledge and accept these facts. Unlike Satan, Job and Isaiah share similarities when they were in God's presence (Isaiah 6:5). Both professed a different view of themselves as well as a radically new view of God. They humbled themselves as a result.

The above truths seem so simple and they are. Yet they are so profound. Their denial and distortion are a carryover from the Garden and God's judgment on Adam and all mankind because of Adam's first sin. Everyone resists, suppresses, and distorts the truth (Romans 1:18-23). They exchange the truth about God and about themselves for a lie. Each person becomes a god to himself and worships the creature — himself — in lieu of the Creator. Every person serves self — to me, for me, by me (anti-Romans 11:36). Every person becomes an idolater in some form and in varying degrees. Only saving and sanctifying grace and the work of the Holy Spirit moves a person from Satan's idolatrous family and kingdom into God's family and kingdom (Colossians 1:13).

Humbly, and I suspect joyfully, Job came to his senses when directly confronted by God. What a testimony! Job and all believers have a gracious, long-suffering Redeemer! Job demanded an audience, but he was not in control. He grew as God's person while in God's discipleship class. Many may be tempted to call Job's demands on God to explain Himself and give an accounting as *understandable*. However, Job was unmasked and exposed as sinful and his responses as rebellious. In the end, Job agreed with God. He repented but not for the reasons or motivation given by his three friends. He tasted God and he was changed forever.

Application

1. What brought about Job's change?

2. Job came to his senses on what basis?

3. God referred to His majesty, power, and beauty by pointing to nature. He used nature to encourage Abraham in terms of God's covenantal faithfulness (Genesis 13:14-17; 22:17).

   a. What is your view of nature?

   b. How do the Psalms (19:1; 50:6; 89:5-6; 97:6) help you view God as Creator and Controller?

   c. What is that significance?

4. Relationships matter. Job was grieved and vexed that he was a friend of God but God was not acting like one.

   a. How do those facts help you understand the cross?

   b. How does Job's story help you in whatever circumstance God has placed you? Please be specific. Move over?

CHAPTER 16
God's Meeting with Job: Part III

JOB CAME TO HIS SENSES as recorded in chapters 40 and 42. He saw himself in the mirror of the truth of God and found himself wanting. Yet he was overjoyed. Relationships do matter! He now knew his relationship with God and God's relationship with him were intact. Circumstances did not change those facts. Circumstances often express what God promised: curses for trusting in self and blessings for trusting in God (Deuteronomy 28 and Leviticus 26). Yet God often delays both the curses and the blessings in this life but never eternally. Such was the concern of the psalmist in Psalm 73. Such was Job's concern (21:1-34 especially verses 6-15, 17, 19, 28-30). *Why do the wicked live on, growing old, and increasing in power (21:7)?* The wicked do seem to prosper and the "good guys" seem to have problems. Job's high view of God added to his perplexity — *I can't figure God out!* (21:22-26).

Circumstances are the stage in which God and people expressed their covenantal faithfulness or unfaithfulness. Job learned that circumstances must be interpreted from God's perspective. Otherwise the cross can be misinterpreted. Jesus was not getting what he deserved except as the perfect Substitute to satisfy the Triune God's redemptive plan and God's justice. Job and the three friends would have considered the cross as a testimony to Christ's innate sinfulness. Rather, the cross points to Christ's goodness, greatness, and Godness!

Circumstances always serve God's purposes. In retrospect, Job's unpleasantness was only for a time. It was a time of discovery and growth. He had discovered the pearl of great price even though he was not looking for it. The pearl was God Himself, His relationship with Job, and Job's relationship with God.

Job was not like the prodigal son who grew disgusted when he was regulated to communing and eating with pigs. The prodigal son came to himself — he came to his senses and returned to the father (Luke 15:17-18). Job also came to his senses but only after a direct encounter with God. Job did not counsel himself as did the Prodigal and Asaph (see Psalm 73:16-18). All three men looked at God's providence at work in their lives. All were oppressed. They were under the circumstances because they viewed God and self through their circumstances and what they had and did not want or what others had that they wanted. They learned to view the circumstances and self through the grid of God and His truth because God gives the circumstances and the resources to get victory in them.

When both Job and Asaph came into the presence of God, their thoughts and desires changed (Psalm 73:16-17; Job 38-42). They were able to interpret themselves, others, and God's providence from God's perspective. They had a proper vertical perspective (Colossians 3:1-3; 1 John 3:1-3). They were released from bondage to self. The truth set them free (John 8:31-23)! They rejoiced as did the prodigal when he came into his father's presence (Luke 15:20-24)!

In Job's case, he initially wanted to argue his case before God sure of his innocence (13:3,6; 16:21). But as he remained in his situation God was distant and He did not answer. Job then declared that God was treating him as an enemy and adversary. Job assumed God was not pursuing him and called for his day in court (19:1-29; 31:35-37; 33:12-18; 40:2). Instead, God took him to His court as the one who must give an account. This was the best and most loving thing God could have done for him. In effect. God led him to the cross. The book of Job has a judicial overtone as I have pointed out. In the last four chapters God addressed Job's judicial demands by giving Job Himself and a proper foundation to understand Christ and the cross.

Job's words are recorded in 42:3: *Surely I spoke about things that I did not understand, things too wonderful for me to know.* Job acknowledged that he spoke from the perspective of limited knowledge (See 38:2 and God's question). Further, he said: I spoke about things too wonderful for me. The word translated wonderful is translated as marvelous in Job 37:5 (see Psalms 71:17; 72:18; 86:10; 96:3; 98:1). Job had been escorted into the heavenly realm as he heard directly from God (37:22; 38:4; 40:6).

The incomprehensible God had condescended and personally conversed with Job. It was a one-sided conversation and Job did not die! Job got God and he left satisfied!

Return to the description of Job's radical change as described in Job 42:5-6. Job said he closed his mouth now that his heart had been opened. Imagine Job sitting before God with ongoing physical problems. As you read the discourse between Job and Elihu and as you read God's presentation of Himself to Job, you should be mesmerized by the conversation and Job's silence before Elihu and God. God poured out the truth about Himself and Job made no mention of his present or past problems. He listened and he made no demands! Job was focused on God. Job could and did function in a God-honoring manner in the "heat of the times." Grace and the Holy Spirit sustained him as he sustained himself. He came to a new and joyful realization that God is awesome and passed finding out by the use of natural, human reasoning and wisdom.

God has no counselors not even Job and certainly not Satan (Isaiah 40:18, 25; Romans 11:33-36). God revealed Himself to Job such that Job's attention was fully on God. He soaked in the truth of God and it penetrated into his inner man and the very fabric of his being. Not only was Job in God's presence, he was a listener and learner. In that way he imitated Christ. Christ made known the Father's will because He was discipled by Him (John 1:14, 18; 4:34; 5:19, 30; 6:35ff,

46; 8:26; 12:49-50). As a result Job understood God and His providence in a way that he had not. He understood God as the Incomprehensible Creator and Controller Who cares for His people. Relationships do matter! He had no business making demands on God. Previously arrogant and ignorant, this man of God humbled himself before God as God paraded Himself and His majesty before Job.

Job's only logical response was recorded in Job 42:6: *Therefore I despise myself and repent in dust and ashes.* Job judged himself and declared his verdict. He had spoken as a fool but now he was speaking as a wise person. Compared to God, there was no comparison in terms of knowledge and wisdom. Make no mistake, Job's new-found understanding was from the inside-out and simply awesome. Now Job understood that the disparity between man's wisdom and God's wisdom is not simply quantitative or even qualitative. God is *sui generis* — in a class by Himself and He is the class Maker! Although man, both unbeliever and believer, knows God, he does not know Him as he ought (Romans 1:18-20). Job had been put into his proper place and he relished the change. God desires all of His children to joyfully humble themselves which proud people do not do (James 4:6-10; 1 Peter 5:5-7).

Job acknowledged the incomprehensibility of God. God's knowledge and Job's knowledge were not even on the same playing field. God is God and Job is not. He assumed God owed him. He was wrong. Job the man of integrity, blameless and upright was coming to grips with God's greatness. He understood himself more clearly. Job grew in fear of the Lord which is the beginning of wisdom and God's design for His people (Proverbs 1:7; Ecclesiastes 12:13-14).

The word used for repent, *nacham*, is not the typical word for repent which is *shuv*. Some have said that Job did not repent, in part, because he did not have anything to repent of. Yet, as I have demonstrated, judicial language is prevalent throughout the book. God chastens Job after asking him who he thinks he is bringing charges against God — *contending* with, *correcting*, and *accusing* God (40:2). Job did take God to task and I believe wanted to take God to court. The book of Job is less about the problem of evil and more about a believer properly responding to God and His providence.

Earlier Job complained of increasing darkness almost a return to primordial chaos and darkness — life was miserable and it seemed to Job that God was at war with him (Genesis 1:1-2; Job 3:4-6, 19; 10:22; 17:12-13; 19:8-12; 26:7-10; 30:28). In chapter 38-41, God used the creation motif to get Job's attention. And it did! Jesus told the disciples in John 16:20-24 that their sorrow would turn to joy. God promoted the reality of joy within the context of hard times (Philippians 3:1; 4:1, 4-6). Such it was with Job. Once Job stopped keeping score, and demanding and charging God, he breathed in the joy of his and God's salvation (Jonah 2:10).

Most often the word *nacham* refers to God (Genesis 6:6-7; Exodus 32:14; Judges 2:18; 1 Samuel 15:11; Jeremiah 18:7-10). The word is a powerful word. Literally, it indicates deep breathing from deep-seated angst often associated with sorrow and remorse within. In Job's case, I believe the word indicated the radical inner-man change within Job. Coming to grips with oneself is often trying and unpleasant to say the least. Job had a radically new view of himself because he had a radically new view of God. What a wonderful display of God's grace. Again, Job rediscovered that relationships do matter! Contrary to Job's feelings and understanding, God had not left Job. Job was able to come to his senses because God did not leave him or forsake him. Job changed his thoughts and desires about God and himself. Proper God-pleasing actions followed.

Chapter 42 closes on an amazing note. Job functioned as a priest for his household. Job had offered sacrifices for his children and now God had him to do the same for his friends (Job 1:5; 42:7-9). God restored Job as His man. He interceded for the friends who had suggested his sacrifices for his children had been a waste (Job 4:7-8; 8:20). I suspect they humbled themselves when they presented to Job their sacrifice and they accepted Job as their priest.

God cleared Job in the sense that Job had spoken rightly about God but they had not (42:8). Job came to know important truths. First, relationships matter and that circumstances do not always indicate what they seem. Second, hard times come on believers and unbelievers and hard times don't discriminate between the two. Third, hard times come to God's people without a relation to their piety. However, God expects and equips believers to use hard times for growth in Christ. The unbeliever can't and won't do this. He only rails at God and often uses God's providence as justification for his dishonoring God.

When Job brought these truths to himself in his audience with God, initially he failed to humble himself (40:2-5). Now in chapter 42, Job is a humbled and humble man. Job was to function not only as a prophet but now God had him function as intercessor and priest. The three friends benefitted from Job's classroom experience!

Ironically, according to the reasoning of the three friends, the cross and God's wisdom were non-existent in the context of Job's problems (1 Corinthians 1:18-31). According to the common logic of the day, since bad things happened to Christ, Christ must change and repent. Circumstances proved that Christ must be out of God's will. He or His parents must have sinned. Such is the thought expressed in Isaiah 53:4, Luke 13:1-5, and John 9:1-4. Losers can't be winners! The cross contrasts the wisdom of God with the "wisdom" of the world (1 Corinthians 1:18-31). Job was experiencing the reality of this contrast.

Job was a type of Christ, but he was not Christ. The sinless Christ never repented. He grieved over sinners and sin both of which point to the eternal counsel of the Triune God (John 6:37-43). Jesus knew the "plan" and His part in that plan. What a plan it was! It was beyond human comprehension. It was simply divine! As had the prophets, Jesus called for the people of Israel to repent. (Matthew 3:2; 4:17; Mark 1:15; See the gospel of Luke 13:1-5, 34-35; 19:41-44; 23:28-31). Eventually, Job grieved over his sin and assumed priestly activities on behalf of his friends. Perhaps he called people to understand and repent. Chapter 42 of the book of Job closes with the people at a worship service. Job had come full circle — sacrifices for his children (1:5) and now sacrifices for family and friends.

It was only after Job's repentance and the completion of the worship service that God blessed Job physically and materially. We assume that his body was healed. The blessings that God bestowed upon Job and his family are a picture of the bounty that God has for every one of His children and His Church. The believer may not receive the bounty this side of heaven but he will at some point (Hebrews 11:39-40). In the meantime, he has God or better, God has him.

Application

1. How is it possible to come into the presence of the living God?

   a. What does that look like?

   b. What are the results?

2. Define repentance.

3. How do you explain Job's repentance and what is its essential ingredient?

4. Does the fact that Job repented indicate that Satan won?

5. Is it possible for Satan to win the cosmic war (see Genesis 3:15; Romans 16:20; Colossians 2:14-15; 1 John 3:8)?

6. Even though the New Testament (James 5:11) lauds Job for his perseverance, the book of Job pictured Job as a broken and joyless man before God restored him. What was Job's perseverance and what sustained him?

7. Give examples of your Job-like activity in terms of making demands on God including calling Him to court.

   a. How has you reading and understanding of Job been a blessing to you?

   b. How have you changed? Please be specific.

CHAPTER 17

Job's Knowledge of the Gospel

EARLIER I NOTED THAT THE *Scriptures foresaw that God would justify the Gentiles by faith and announced the gospel in advance to Abraham* (Galatians 3:8). Abraham received the gospel message. Earlier I asked how much Job knew in regards to the gospel. Four particular passages in the book of Job seem to refer to an anticipated Redeemer. These include Job 9:33-34; 16:19; 19:25; and 33:23-24. The figure of a mediator or arbiter appears in these passages but what is his nature. Understanding the concept of a mediator between God and Job may have provided Job with hope and the assurance that he would be heard. A real question centers on how these passages should be interpreted now. Should they be interpreted strictly from a New Testament fulfillment point of view? What kind of Christological focus should the reader draw? Do these four passages help us determine Job's level of understanding of the gospel? In the following paragraphs I try to answer some of those questions.

The first text is found in Job 9:33-34: *If only there were someone to arbitrate between us, to lay hands upon us both, someone to remove God's rod from me, so that his terror might frighten me no more.* Chapters 9-10 of the book of Job contain Job's second response. Eliphaz's words in 5:1 are fresh in Job's ears: *Call if you will, but who will answer you; to which of the holy ones will you turn?* Bildad has just spoken in chapter 8 and concluded the chapter with the assurance that God does not reject the blameless or bless the evil doer but he is sure Job must repent (8:20-22). Job had a high view of God which added to his problem with God — how can it be that he is in this condition (9:22-24; 21:22-26). God is awesome and transcendent by nature and now He seemed so far away. Job desired someone to intervene on his behalf, someone who would help him argue his case in court.

Job's speech recorded in chapters 9-10 is laced with forensic terms and courtroom imagery such that he wants answers (9:3, 14-16, 19-20, 24, 32-33; 10:2, 17). He wondered what charges God had made against him. Job desired to establish his case and innocence before God. I suspect one of his motivations was to get out of his situation — RELIEF!

Verse 11 contains an interesting phrase: *When he passes me, I cannot see him . . .* Job, as are others, is referring to the demonstration of God's presence (see Exodus 33:19; 1 Kings 19:11; Mark 6:48). Job concluded that God was great — so transcendent — that Job's relationship with God and his innocence (which was correct) was of no benefit to him. Later in chapter 9, Job desired someone to arbitrate between he and God because he was not confident God would take the time and hear him, let alone answer him (9:3, 14-15). He despised his own life (7:16; 9:21) out of hopelessness and uncertainty based on a wrong view of God and hard providences. In 42:6, Job despised himself because he had come face to face with God and God *set him straight.*

The original word translated as arbitrate is a common word in the book of Job and has a judicial, forensic tone (see above and 5:17; 6:25-26; 13:3, 10, 15; 22:4; 40:2). It is translated as judge, prove, rebuke, punish, accuse, argue, correct, instruct, and defend. The references refer to Job's questions and or charges to and against God, Eliphaz's contention that God brings charges against Job (22:4), and God's charge against Job for taking Him to court (40:2). Early in the book, it seems that for the most part Job is making a plea. He wants an umpire, a go-between. Early in the book, Job may not be seeking justice and vindication as much as an answer from God. Job did not understand how God could be treating him this way — unjustly, warlike fashion, as his enemy when as far as he knew his relationship with God and God with him was intact, and as an expression of God's abuse of His power (13:24; 19:8-11; 24:1-12; 30:29; 33:10-11). Later in the book, Job brings specific charges against God (19:6; 31:35; 40:3-5; 42:3). We do know he is seeking understanding in the areas of reconciliation and relational restoration but as so often happens in the midst of hard times personal demands outstrip humble reliance on God and His grace.

Job has spoken in relational terms (Job 9:2-3 — 6:2-7, 8-13). He affirms his innocence and is unaware that he has offended God (6:10; 9:2-3, 14-15; 16:17; 27:6); to Job, his innocence does not count with God. Job also acknowledged God's "far-awayness" and believed he needed help to "get to God." One of his overriding desires was to know if his relationship with God was intact. If it wasn't, he wanted God to tell him how his relationship could be restored. His circumstances — God's providence — were proof to him and others that his relationship with God and God with him was fractured. Therefore for all these reasons Job was sure he needed an arbiter. Our passage in chapter 9 may or may not refer to Christ. It may simply be that Job was looking for a friend who would act in his behalf. He had not found one. We can't say for sure that he was or was not looking for Christ. However, he was looking for help outside of himself.

The second text is found in Job 16:18-22: *O earth do not cover my blood; may my cry never be laid to rest; Even now my witness is in heaven; my advocate is on high; My intercessor is my friend as my eyes pour out tears to God; on behalf of a man he pleads with God as a man pleads with a friend. Only a few years will pass before I go on the journey of no return.* Job in the preceding verses (v. 15-17) summarized his misery. Apparently Job thought he would not be vindicated before his peers. He perceived he had little time on this earth. His only hope was a friend (advocate, intercessor, witness) in heaven. Who is this witness in heaven? Some may say

Christ. Others such as John Calvin thought that Job was referring to his own good case. Job had a good case and it seemed that God agreed since He declared Job's integrity in the Prologue (1:1, 3, 8; 2:3). Did Job believe that he could stand before God at some point and present his own case? Did he believe that he would have the opportunity to act as his own lawyer? Early on, he was worn down by false counsel and his condition did not change. He earnestly desired and later demanded an audience with God. He got one but he did not speak until he had made a proper examination of himself based on a proper understanding of God (Job 40:3-5; 42:6; 2 Corinthians 13:5).

The third text is well-known and is found in Job 19:25-27: *I know that my Redeemer lives and that in the end I will stand upon the earth. And after my skin has been destroyed yet in my flesh I will see God. I myself will see him with my own eyes — I and not another. How my heart yearns within me!* Who is the identity of this mediator — redeemer? Is Job giving a picture of resurrection life purchased by the mediatorial work of a crucified and risen Christ? We can say that Job had a firm belief in a God who hears. But that belief, which is true, only perplexed him given his continued problems (21:22-26). According to Job, his God was silent and perhaps absent. Why hadn't God offered an explanation? Why was God silent? Job believed that his case would not fall on deaf ears, but he wanted God to hurry up — listen and answer.

The word translated Redeemer is *goel*. Most likely the word referred to the work of God as a friend and kinsman who will be a blessing to Job (see the book of Ruth). It is likely that Job perceives that blessing being received as he is redeemed from the dust of death. Job's emphasis is not on redemption from guilt and judgment (the most common Hebrew term for this is *padah*). He is looking forward to an advocate in heaven on his behalf who will vindicate him and all of God's faithful servants before the world.

The passages before us are expressions of Job's hope that motivated him to endure and persevere (James 5:11). How much he envisioned a crucified and perhaps resurrected Christ is unknown. Job must have had some idea of the cross and life after death. Still with that understanding he demanded God to give him an audience. In that sense he lived the lie. But at other times, his endurance was not a mere "suck-it-up." Rather Job, as should all believers, again at times especially early on was able to look heavenward with an apparent eternal focus. However, he was confused and lived for a time by sight and not by saving faith (14:18-22; 21:22-26). The three friends gave answers for this life but not the next. They were a burden rather than a blessing for Job.

The last text is found in Job 33:23-24: *Yet if there is an angel on his side as a mediator, one out of a thousand, to tell a man what is right for him, to be gracious to him and say, "Spare him from going down to the pit; I have found a ransom for him . . .* Elihu described an angelic mediator or perhaps simply a messenger (Job refers to this in 9:32-35). In verses 23-28 of chapter 33, Elihu may be referring to God's redemptive purpose especially in hard providence (trials).The words "restored by God to his righteous state" in verse 26 may refer to a right standing before God, secured in and by God, or it could simply refer to a former condition such as Job had before God or could refer to a standard of right and wrong.

On the other hand, the context seemed to be a quest for the answer to what is the righteousness of man. Job wanted to know his good case so that he could present it and himself to God. Ironically, Job could have presented God's own testimony about Job if God had revealed it to him (1:1, 8; 2:3). God had given His view of Job. However, God's words were unknown to Job. Job's understanding of his relationship with God and Job's circumstances didn't seem to be in sync according to the theology of the day as expounded by the friends. On the other hand, could it be possible that the author of the book is alluding to justification by faith: God's imparted righteousness that comes as a gift through the Holy Spirit received by saving faith. Earlier, I suggested that justification by faith was known in some form to Job but obviously only in nascent and limited form.

God placed these four passages in the book of Job to benefit His people. On this side of the cross, the Church and believers must develop the ability to look back and look forward (1

Corinthians 10:1-4; 1 Timothy 1:12-16; Philippians 3:12-14). Believers must place themselves in the setting of earlier saints. Evaluating God's word from their perspective given their level of understanding and God's revelation is humbling, instructive, and hope-engendering. The Old Testament was written for our instruction. Such is the case made in the following passages: Romans 4:23-24; 15:1-6, 13-15; 1 Corinthians 1:8-10; 10:6, 11; and 2 Timothy 3:15-17.

It is quite humbling and hope-generating to know that the Triune God has always provided truth through the ages. He sent the Son to explain the Father and His ways (John 1:14, 18). The Holy Spirit illumines the heart, provides insight into God's will for His people, and showers the believer with enabling and sanctifying grace so that truth is applied. We can conclude that Job had some inkling of the Messiah and perhaps life after death and even resurrection life. God did not reveal the fullness of His redemptive plan to Job but Job did not need this. Job had all he needed for life and godliness (2 Peter 1:3-4). Job had to grow and grow he did. Job had to learn to focus on what he knew about God and himself rather than demand that which was not his (Deuteronomy 29:29).

God revealed Himself, not necessarily His ways, to Job more fully in chapters 38-41. In response, Job turned his attention from self. He continued to humble himself and he repented. God ministered to Job by simply revealing Himself as God and Job as the creature. The divide between God and Job and between God and man was bridged by God by establishing, maintaining, and growing proper relationships. For those of us on this side of the cross, we need to reevaluate our approach to God and His providence. Again I think one major key in the book of Job is our response to God in the context of God's hard providence. Being in Christ and knowing God in Christ by the Holy Spirit was a key for Job even in rudimentary form. It should be a fuller and more thrilling blessing for all believers this side of the cross.

Application

1. Embedded in the Old Testament are truths that are more fully revealed in the New Testament. What is in the Old Testament is revealed more fully in the New Testament and what is in the New Testament is concealed in the Old Testament.

   a. From the book of Job, what do you learn about God and His method of revelation?

   b. What is revealed to Job that anticipated Christ's first coming (see John 1:1-5, 6-11, 14, 18)?

2. What does Christ as the visible image of the invisible God and God's final revelation mean to you?

   a. John 14:6-9: *if you have seen Me you have seen the Father.* What is Jesus referring to?

b. Also see John 1:14, 18; Hebrews 1:1-3 in order to answer.

3. Job had knowledge of God but he did not know God as he ought.

a. God was past finding out — he was incomprehensible. What does that mean?

b. How was that a blessing and burden to Job?

c. The truth of Scripture simplifies life. Explain. See John 8:31-32.

d. How was Job blessed? What did he learn about himself and what did he learn about God and His ways?

CHAPTER 18

Mini-Review, Summary, and Satan

As NOTED IN THE INTRODUCTION, the four subtitles are a partial summary of the book. Job had lost sight of these truths or he had not known them from the beginning. He did focus on these truths at the end of the book. Joyful trust, obedience, and blessings followed.

God's sovereignty, the first S should not be limited to His power. In His wisdom and control, God is powerful, purposeful, and good — all the time. God knows, He plans, He ordains, and He brings all things to pass for His glory and the good of His people. God's business is glorifying the Triune God. These are non-negotiable, indisputable truths. Denying or ignoring them is God-denying, which is dangerous, misleading, and leads to more misery.

As noted previously but worth repeating, one author expressed these truths in this way: God is completely sovereign — He always wills what is best; God is infinite in wisdom — He always knows what is best; God is perfect in love — He has the power to bring it about (page 18; *Trusting God: Even When Life*

Hurts; Jerry Bridges; Navpress. Colorado Springs, Colorado). Initially, Job acknowledged God's power in terms of control, but he did not agree that God was good, wise, or purposeful. Job's definition of good differed from God's definition. Many may agree that God is powerful but not good. Or they will contend that God is good but not powerful. In either case, the person sets himself up as judge and jury as he takes God to court. Joyless misery follows.

Suffering, the second S, focuses on a believer's experience of and response to God's providence. As I have mentioned several times, culture and Christians tend to import subjectivity into the word suffering. In the original language of the Greek New Testament, *pascho* and its roots are commonly translated as suffering, affliction, and trouble. The words indicate a person's experience and life situations and not his response. They are descriptions of God's providence and are the context of the person's response to God. A response to God's providence is a response to God. Moreover, experiences, trouble, affliction, however defined, don't change a person. They may influence thoughts, desires, and actions but they are not causative. In addition, thinking, wanting, and acting are patterned. They are "natural" because they have been practiced.

From another perspective, circumstances as well as all facts are neutral. Many will disagree but facts will be and must be interpreted. Every person employs various and multiple interpretative girds such as feelings; thoughts about self, God, and others; and wants and desires when faced with any circumstances. The circumstance itself does not control a person's response. Job learned that he is not a victim to and of God and His providence — His power and control. Rather, people respond and change in the context of God's providence. One's view of God, self, and providence determine one's response.

As a person changes his view of God and of self, his response to God, others, and God's providence will change. Such was the case with Job. When the Christian imports subjectivity into the situation, he takes and will continue to take his focus off God and His purpose. As a result, he becomes increasingly self-focused. The person opts to focus on control by him, for him, and to him thereby competing with God.

The third S is suspicion. Job was suspicious of God. He asked what God was doing and later he demanded that God give him an accounting. The friends were suspicious of Job but they were not suspicious of themselves.

The fourth S is success. God's definition of success differed from that of Job and the three friends. In the end, God was honored and glorified. Job joyfully and tearfully humbled himself. He was restored and comforted. He grew in his love and adoration of God. The three friends and others were restored because of Job's ministry. We assume the friends repented. Satan was revealed for who and what he is.

We have made a quick excursion through the book of Job. We encountered God in the heavens surrounded by His agents and minions. In the prologue (chapters 1-2), we witnessed an extraordinary scene: Satan defiantly, arrogantly, and ignorantly in God's presence. He was unconcerned about his eternal destiny. It was only by God's design in the unseen world that Satan was in God's presence! Some may quibble with the phrase "the ignorance of Satan." We must "move" further back in "history" to obtain an accurate picture of Satan's activity in a good God's world.

At same point, all the angels experienced the pristine presence of God. But they were not privy to all that God knew and ordained. When the earth was created, apparently all of the angels were there to sing praises to God, the Creator (Job 38:7; Psalm 148:2-3). Specifically, Job was not there. Therefore, he should not have expected, let alone demanded, to know God's plans for the world, mankind, and himself. He must be content with what God has revealed (Deuteronomy 29:29).

Rebelliously, Satan attempted to place himself on a par with, even above, God. In response, God exiled Satan and his followers. Satan has continued to attempt to gather followers, but his efforts are doomed to failure (Genesis 3:15; Romans 16:20, 25-27). It is noteworthy that God uses satanic activity as His tool to bring people to Himself and to grow them individually and as a body, the Church (see 2 Samuel 24:1 and 1 Chronicles 21:1; Matthew 16:23; Ephesians 4:11-15).

Specifically, Satan attempted to use God's people against God as in the case of Job. Job was not Satan's target — God was! He tried to convince God that He had to buy Job in order to keep Job fearing Him (1:9-11; 2:5-6). Satan attempted to use Job against God. One can only wonder if Satan really thought he could win and outdo God. From the start, Satan's intentions were arrogant, ignorant, and self-serving. Little did he realize, or perhaps more accurately acknowledge, that he was under God's authority in heaven and on earth. Unwittingly, Satan was making a vague reference to the cross: every believer has been bought with a price! Once paid, the payment will never be revoked (Romans 8:1, 34; 11:28-30; Hebrews 7:25)!

Satan was convinced that God could not keep His people. Perhaps he was reflecting on his own fall. Perhaps he blamed God for his fall! With enough pressure applied to Job, Satan was convinced that God would be demonstrated as an impotent failure. Satan challenged God to remove His hedge (protection: 1:9) from Job by removing the pleasures of life including Job's physical health. Ironically, Satan had offered the pleasures of God's good Garden to Eve which were not his to offer for the purpose of using them against God. Satan must have been certain of what he considered were the fickleness and shallowness of God's friendship and provisions in the Garden and His saving work in believers.

Satan "chose" Job, a type of Christ, to be the poster boy for God's presumed and hoped-for failure as a Savior, Comforter, and Deliverer. However, God was using Satan and the three friends to highlight His presence, goodness, and mercy as well as His power and justice. Once Job humbled himself and knowledge of himself and God was clarified, joy returned to Job, his household, and friends. The joy was based on a proper understanding of relationships. Job did not envision going down in order to go up. In the end, Job remained a man of integrity, but he was not the same person at the end of the book. He grew in the simple truth that God is God and he is not. He had had the rights and privileges of a child of God and the King, but he had not used them well.

Application

1. Review the four "S" and write out their significance to Job and to you.

2. What do you learn about Satan? Why is that important?

3. What is God's "antidote" against satanic influence? See John 8:31-32, 2 Corinthian 10:3-5, and 1 John 5:18-20.

4. What truths are taught in Psalm 119:9-11 and how do they apply to you?

CHAPTER 19

The Incomprehensibility of God: Part I

JOB WAS FACED WITH THE incomprehensible God. Job had unwittingly attempted to bring God down to his level. He thought God owed him. A radical "about-face" occurred in Job. Throughout the book he was introduced to the truth that God answers in His time. Job learned clearly that God owes no one anything. Moreover, the book of Job resoundingly proclaims that relationships matter. God is trustworthy and faithful to Himself, to His promises, and to His people in that order. He will never forsake His people because He is true to Himself and He has forsaken His Son once for all in order to accomplish the purpose of the Triune God. Therefore, His people, in the Old and New Testaments can and should expect God to remain faithful to Himself and to His promises (1 Corinthians 1:8-9; 10:13; 2 Corinthians 1:22; 5:5; 1 Thessalonians 5:24). The cross looks backwards and forward. This is the best news yet! The cross, the resurrection, and the outpouring of the Holy Spirit affirm the Triune's God's trustworthiness as He works out His eternal plan of salvation (John 6:37-43).

You might be thinking: Job did not know that! True if you mean in its fullest form. As I have discussed, Job did know the gospel as did Abraham (Galatians 3:8). All the patriarchs and God's people had some understanding that God is the Promisemaker and Promisekeeper. God had declared Himself so and He has given Himself to His people and holds them to His bosom. God had Job but Job did not believe that fact. Initially, Job perceived only darkness, death, and despair. He cursed the day of his birth and his continued existence (3:1-10, 11-19, 20-26).

To reiterate, Job was guided by circumstances, experiences, feelings, and his understanding of God and self. He read God from these four pillars rather than beginning with God and moving to self, others, and experiences. Man's experiences are not simply life or life events but God's providential control being played out daily.

Job grew as a theologian both in terms of knowledge of self and of God and in faith. Faith and knowledge are always linked. Saving faith seeks understanding; reason seeks saving faith and faithful understanding; and faith and reason strengthened one another (Romans 4:20-21). Job felt alone but he was not. His feelings and his friends were not helpful; feelings rarely are and false counsel never is. Job relied on feelings rather than on basic fundamental truths. He jettisoned them as he waited but without hope or only with a *hope-so* (1 Thessalonians 4:13). Living by feelings is always a control issue for everyone even believers.

As I have said and will repeat, Job learned that feelings, reason divorced from biblical truth, and experience as standards for thoughts, desires, and actions are no match for reliance on God and His word. They never trump God's truth and when followed, only lead to misery and strife (Proverbs 5:21-22; 13:15b; 26:11).

We know that the gospel was presented beforehand to Abraham. I suspect this was not an isolated event because Job lived in the patriarchal period. How much Job knew of the gospel and resurrection life we aren't told. We know that Job was torn within his very being. Inner-man angst was fueled by his wrong thinking about God and himself. However, after being in the presence of God, Job took to heart God's exposition of His creative power as evidenced in inanimate and animate creation (Job 38-42). God's power was unlimited except by the very nature and person of God. Moreover, the wisdom of God took on a new dimension for Job. God's thoughts and ways had not been Job's thoughts and ways (Isaiah 55:8-9). Job eventually embraced truth and grew in his understanding and appreciation of God as defined in Job 40 and 42. Job's thoughts and desires became more like God's. Job confessed and repented of his sin of arrogance and ignorance. Satan had no such desire or movement in that direction. You can only wonder how Satan responded to God's victory in Job.

God's acceptance of Job's confession and repentance is not stated as such. Based on the events that follow, we know it was.

We are not told of Satan's response, of the destiny of Job's wife, or of Job's healing. We are told that God had Job intercede as His priest on behalf of the three counselors. The three friends were to supply the animals for the sacrifice. Job's priestly work would cost the three friends. Nothing is free as demonstrated by the Levitical sacrificial system. The Israelite man as head of the house was to bring to the priest an unblemished male animal without defect and cut its throat. The priest would step in and offer the blood sacrifice. This was a preview of Christ's once-for-all sacrifice (Hebrews (6:19-20; 7:11-12, 26-28; 9:11-14; 10:1-4, 19-22).

Job was restored and God brought back Job's family, who apparently had alienated themselves from Job, the previously prosperous and caring patriarch (Job 19:13-20). All of his family was forgiven, and they came and consoled, comforted, and rejoiced with him (42:10-12).

Most importantly for the Church and individual believers, God vindicated Himself! The cross and the resurrection are the ultimate affirmations of God's Godness! You may wonder if God grows weary of declaring and revealing Himself. Jesus faced this same weakness of faith in those who were or would be His true people. He came to his own (the nation of Israel) but they rejected Him (John 1:5, 9-11). The disciples did not get it (John 14:6-9). Very few people accepted the truth that Jesus was God, the Messiah — until the outpouring of the Holy Spirit (Acts 2). However, God's children, like Job, will eventually comprehend and be energized by true facts. A fundamental fact for all believers is the Being of God and what He has done in Christ and is doing by the Holy Spirit.

The faithfulness and trustworthiness of God are bedrock pillars of truth. Circumstances and experience (God's providence), feelings, and human understanding divorced from biblical truth don't negate these truths. Seeking to understand God and His ways may be a blessing or a curse. However, knowing God and His ways are privileges and blessings that every believer has. Believers must learn to use their divinely-designed seeking capacity in a God-pleasing way (Proverbs 2:1-10; Matthew 6:33).

Initially Job was not satisfied. He sought and he sought. His understanding sought faith but not necessarily growth in saving faith. He was not thinking God's thoughts. He would not correctly understand the cross until his encounter with the God. He knew relationships mattered but he was drowning in a tsunami of feelings unchecked by biblical truth and the buoyancy of a working, growing faith. What Job did not know was the depth of God's relationship with him. He lacked understanding of the true God and himself. Believers on this side of the cross have a similar problem. Among other truths, the cross highlights the importance of relationships.

Relationships began in eternity past and are Intratrinitarian by design and fulfillment. The cross grows out of the divine plan to magnify God and His goodness and power. Unless man looks to and climbs toward the heights of God's majesty and glory, God will not be fully magnified (Philippians 3:7-11). Unless man plumbs the depths and fullness of the sinfulness of mankind and the wickedness of sin, God will not be fully magnified (Ephesians 1:15-23; 3:14-21). The depth of God's glory is as deep as His love, mercy, justice, and wrath. The cross magnifies those truths because it magnifies the Triune God (1 Corinthians 1:18-23). The believer will stumble like Job and demand God to perform by explaining Himself. Sadly, for the believer with that mindset, the cross and the outpouring Holy Spirit will be insufficient for godly living.

Such it was with Job. He knew relationships mattered. He assumed his relationship with God and God's with him was non-existent or insufficient to avoid his trouble. He wondered what it would take for his relationship to be reestablished with God. At least he sought God for the answer.

In the end, with resounding and joyful clarity, Job discovered that God's relationship with him had not changed. Circumstances had changed but not God's relationship with Job. God placed Job in the position in which the *why* of God's activity was hidden. Job believed God had forsaken him. God had not. Job had lived a lie and suffered the consequences. Job never received the *why* of God's activities. In the end, Job was satisfied with God without the knowledge that Job had demanded. Having God was far superior to having answers to his demands. His questions were answered *yes* in Christ and the Holy Spirit (2 Corinthians 1:20-22). Being forgiven was far better than having answers to his questions. In fact, Job did have answers: God is God and he is not. And that was best for Job!

Application

1. Relationships matter. How did that fact play out in Job's life?

2. Summarize your relationship with God and His with you.

   a. What are the joys of each?

   b. What are the areas that you need growth?

3. God has all the answers for any and all questions that anyone could ask but God may withhold answering.

   a. Give reasons as you study the book of Job.

   b. What is God's final answer (2 Corinthians 1:20-22; 5:5)

4. Satisfaction and contentment depend on what? How did a proper knowledge of God and self lead to both?

5. How would you apply Philippians 2:14-17 to Job and to yourself?

CHAPTER 20

The Incomprehensibility of God: Part II

PREVIOUSLY, I MENTIONED AND SUMMARIZED a major theme and a unifying feature of the book of Job: God's sovereignty and the incomprehensibility of God. The term incomprehensibility of God refers to knowledge of God. The term does not refer to God's knowledge of Himself and of all things. Nothing is incomprehensible to God not even Himself! The following terms are used to help us have some inkling of God's knowledge. It is original, immediate, incommunicable, intuitive, innate, infinite, inexhaustible, absolute, perfect, personal, underived, necessary, eternal, complete and comprehensive. Wow! The multitude of words is an attempt to highlight an attribute or perfection of God — His knowledge. God knows unlike any other because He is God! God knows Himself eternally, completely, totally, and finally. Amazing! God's knowledge is both qualitatively and quantitatively without comparison to all other knowledge of all other beings. Moreover, He is the source of knowledge. Without God, there would be no knowledge.

God is knowable to His creatures which in itself is quite remarkable. But in what ways is He knowable? Theologically, the terms "understanding" and "comprehension" refer to that which is able to be understood but not exhaustively. To say that God is incomprehensible is not to say that God is utterly unknowable to mankind. Man knows Him because man, by God's creative design, is the image of God. As such, man is a rational and moral being — he thinks, desires, and acts. Moreover, man is faith-based, a chooser, and a worshiper all of which requires knowledge and a relationship. God designed man to know Him and to be in His presence. The fall did not negate or remove these truths.

The believer comes into God's presence at salvation via the Holy Spirit, continues in His presence via union with Christ and the indwelling Holy Spirit, and is continuously perfected even in eternity. Salvation on earth begins eternal life via the believer's relationship with the Triune God (John 17:3). Eternal life begins on earth as does resurrection life (Romans 6:9-11; Revelation 1:18), The believer is able to think God's thoughts and desire what God desires. He has been brought into the very presence of God and he did not die. Rather, he entered into a new existence and a new life (Matthew 3:2; 4:17; Mark 1:15; John 1:14-18; 2 Corinthians 5:17)!

Further, man has a God-given moral consciousness and the requirements of the law written on his heart — he knows God (Romans 2:14-15). Further still, God's reveals Himself in creation such that every person is known by God, knows God, and is without excuse (Acts 17:27-28; Romans 1:18-23). Yet man's knowledge of God, pre- and post-fall, has always been limited, finite, and incomplete. Post-fall, man's knowledge of God and self is distorted and man denies the very existence and beauty of God and man as a dependent creature. Adam and Eve, mankind's first parents who initially had a perfect relationship with God also had limited, finite, and incomplete knowledge of God but it was true knowledge without distortion.

Therefore, and I repeat, the term incomprehensibility does not mean that man does not know God in some fashion. It does mean that no man can comprehend God thoroughly, perfectly, or completely. Even believers in heaven will never know God completely or perfectly. Therefore, every person, believer and unbeliever, does not know God as they ought. Man will always be the creature and God the Creator. But believers enjoy learning and the joy of fellowship with the living God!

Man is finite and God is infinite; man is fallen, a sinner, under the curse and condemnation of sin (Romans 1:18-20); and believers "see" God and His glory because Christ is the image and glory of God. Believers see the glory of God only in Christ only via the eyes of saving faith (1 John 3:1-3; 4:11-12; John 1:14, 18; 14:6-9; 2 Corinthians 4:4, 6; 5:7).

In addition, the secret things — those things unrevealed and beyond man's knowledge such as the future and who will be saved — belong to God and not to man. They are God's concern ordained in eternity past. Yet God has chosen to reveal Himself and many things — His law and His revealed will — in His word for His glory and man's good. God has revealed and provided all that the believer needs for life and godliness (2 Peter 1:3-4). But the secret things belong to God (Deuteronomy 29:29).

God is the Revealer but, on His schedule, and not man's. He reveals in terms of principles as well as precepts. He gives His children the knowledge and grace to make specific application of His truth. Man's knowledge of God and himself is linked to saving faith which produces trust, obedience, love, and a desire for the surpassing knowledge of Christ. It is good news that resurrection life begins at salvation so that the believer has a foretaste of heaven (Philippians 3:7-11; Romans 6:9-10; 2 Corinthians 4:13-14; 1 John 3:1-3)!

Based on the above truths, Job knew God as did the three friends and as does every person. Unlike the unbeliever, the believer knows God intimately because God knows him with supreme intimacy. At the same time and for the reasons given above, every person has limited knowledge in general and specifically of God. That knowledge is enough to hold every person accountable before God and the believer to entice him to seek the Light. Man's knowledge in general and of God is temporal, analogical, creaturely, derived, and confused. Yet it is still worthy of every person's attention. The believer will grow in his understanding of God and self. In a real sense, they are no "dummies" in God's kingdom and family.

To say that man is comprehensible means that he can know and be known; he can be known practically and experientially but even knowledge of self or another is limited. Others know man imperfectly and incompletely and man knows himself imperfectly and incompletely. In contrast, God knows Himself perfectly, completely, and eternally and God knows man perfectly, completely, eternally, effortlessly, and comprehensively. God is the great and ultimate Knower. He is past finding out and would remain only a "blur" in the thinking of man unless He has revealed Himself which He has (Psalm 145:3; 147:5). He has revealed in a general way as described above and in special way in His Son and in His word (John 14:6; 17:17).

To say that God is known by man means that He is known in limited measure by finite, sinful man. But the knowledge that man has of God is true knowledge. In another vein, to say that God is incomprehensible is to mean that there is discontinuity between man's thoughts and God's thoughts of Himself and His creation. God's ways and thoughts are not man's thoughts and desires (Isaiah 55:8-9). Man is not God and he is not privy to God's secret thoughts and ways (Deuteronomy 29:29). They will be revealed but on God's schedule and in His way.

The importance of the subject of knowledge is especially demonstrated by Christ and Job. Job came face to face with God's incomprehensibility. He acted upon the premise that God owed him and what God knew, or at least His plans, should be made known to Job. Early on Job's understanding of God was summed up as "God as I know Him and how I expect Him to act." Job did not know God or himself as he thought he did. Job wanted to know his fate, a way out, and an end. He was focused on self and he was more interested in having God explain himself than he was in honoring God. Job came to acknowledge his lack of knowledge and only then did he come to know. But initially Job's knowledge was of the present. It was less about knowing God for who He was so that Job could please Him. Job's lack of understanding of God's ways was a burden to him. He wanted answers for himself and not for the purpose of honoring God.

You might say that the above assessment is too hard. In response, I think one of the beauties of the book of Job is drawing attention to the beauty and the pitfalls of trusting and not trusting God no matter the circumstances. God is trustworthy and the believer is to function as a trusting person. Circumstances, feelings, experience, and knowledge divorced from biblical truth doesn't change that fact. Job did come to trust God but it was only through and after God "befriended" him by giving Job Himself, This fact previews and highlights one lesson of the cross.

Application

1. Define knowledge. It is always linked to faith — saving or non-saving faith.

2. How do you link the two in your life? What are the results?

3. The content of faith, saving or non-saving, is defined as knowledge. Everyone knows something.

   a. How is that fact possible?

   b. Facts and knowledge are not the same. Facts are neutral and must be interpreted. Knowledge is both innate and derived.

      1. What standard do you use to interpret facts?

      2. Where does the Bible fit into your interpretative grid?

4. Truth will set you free; facts don't set you free unless they are based on truth. What is truth?

CHAPTER 21
The Incomprehensibility of God: Part III

IN CONTRAST TO JOB, JESUS knew God and God knew Him (John 10:30). Using an old vernacular, we would say that their relationship was *tight*. Yet there were things that Christ did not make known because that right belonged to the Triune God (Matthew 24:36; Mark 11:12-13; 13:22). Purposefully and correctly, Jesus knew and proclaimed His origin, destiny, and the way back to heaven (John 14:1-3; Hebrews 12:1-3). He never lost sight of His identity, His mission, and His destiny — His "due date" to complete the course and return to the Father. He was motivated by the desire to glorify the Triune God by pleasing the Father. He did this by running the race with endurance and completing His mission (Hebrews 12:1-3).

Job had missed the beauty of securely knowing his destiny and God's holding power. Jesus remembered the end (eternally in God's presence) and the way to the end (a vital relationship with God as the Son of God via the cross) which enabled Him to stay the course as the Victor (Romans 8:35-39). For the believer, growth in gratitude and dependence on his relationship with

God through the Son by the Holy Spirit is manifested by increasing faith, hope, and love in the present life. In that way he imitates Christ. Imitating Christ would have enabled Job to be glad when he was sad (John 16:20-24; Romans 5:1-5; 14:20-21; 1 James 1:2-4; Peter 1:6-7). Long obedience in the same direction requires a proper view of God and His faithfulness based in part on who you are in Christ (1 John 1:5-7).

Job knew that God was a Person, a rational, emotive Being who creates and sustains — He controls! Job knew that God thought and desired and that God's thoughts and desires always come to pass always in His time. In fact, thoughts and desires determine God's action and His providence. We must be careful here. God does not think and desire like man. Man thinks and reasons as a process or in a succession of moments or in the vernacular of neuroanatomy via chemical messengers and firing neurons. There is no process or succession of moments with God. There are no time and space constraints with God. He is the Creator of both!

God is Spirit and as such it is as if God is all thought and all desire at the same time. Moreover, God is Light (1 John 1:5) and creates light (Genesis 1:3). His word is light (Psalm 36:9; 119:105, 130; Proverbs 6:23). Jesus proclaims Himself as the way, truth, life, and light (John 8:12; 9:5; 12:46; 14:6). God has given us a piece of His "mind" — His thoughts and desires in His word. God is the Revealer. Job had some understanding of truth. Therefore,

God blesses, desires, and expects/expected His people in every age to act according to truth.

Job functioned as if he could expect God to function like any other person. Perhaps that is why God providentially brought him five counselors (including his wife) all of whom did not know God as they ought. The whole crew was in God's classroom of knowing and knowledge. Only Job graduated and magna sum laude at that! All believers are growing and are to be growing all the more in this area!

Individuals, as did Job, may function as if they should be privy to God's secret will — to the eternal counsel of the Godhead. When faced with troubles, Job wanted to know God's secret will — His decisions, judgements, and outcomes at least for him. Those are God's. God gives to man what man needs to live as one of His children moment by moment and day by day.

The hymn, *Day by Day* presents it well. It was written by Carolina Sandell Berg a twenty-six year old Swedish girl after her father, a Lutheran pastor in Sweden, drowned. He was thrown overbroad as they traveled across the lake and she witnessed his death. She penned the hymn in 1850 or so and it highlights her approach to God and His hard providences. The hymn highlights God the trustworthy Giver and her response to Him day by day and moment by moment in the midst of God's providence. She finds strength to meet her trials because of relationships: God's with her and hers with God. The hymn gives a mini-picture of God's covenantal faithfulness and a proper response to it. The first stanza gives words to live by that should have been a blessing to Job and for every believer: *Day by day and with each passing moment, strength I find to meet my trials here; trusting in my Father's wise bestowment I've no cause for worry or for fear. He whose heart is kind beyond all measure gives unto each day what he deems best — lovingly, it is part of pain and pleasure, mingling toil with peace and rest.*

However, no matter what man knows regarding decisions, judgments, and outcomes as revealed by God in His Word, man is still without full knowledge of God, himself, and God's providence. However, no believer is without the resources to trust and fear God. They have all they need for life and godliness (1 Corinthians 10:13; 2 Peter 1:3-4).

In many cases knowing the outcome seems to satisfy a person. Knowing the immediate outcome seemed to be Job's goal as it is for many people. However, when having that knowledge becomes a person's driving motivation, the goal to become more like Christ becomes non-existent. When that happens the person is using God. He is not living by faith but by sight. Often God will leave His people in the situation until the person "comes to his senses" which Job, several psalmists, and the prodigal are depicted to have done (Psalm 42:5, 11; 43:1; 73:16-19; Luke 15:17-18). All believers eventually come to their senses although in varying degrees and at varying times in this life.

Job knew God but he did not know God as He truly is. This fact became clear as recorded in Job 40:3-5 and 42:1-6. Because of God's design of man — he is the image of God — God has plans for man. Post-fall, part of God's design is growth in Christlikeness. Only Christ is the perfect image of God (2 Corinthians 4:4; Colossians 1:15; Hebrews 1:1-3). Only He knows God as He truly is; only He reveals the Father as He is (John 1:18; 14:6-9; 2 Corinthians 4:4, 6). When the believer is becoming more like Christ, he is glorifying God and he enters into God's presence and enjoys God through the gift and use of saving faith (1 John 3:1-3). Relationships matter!

Job was not where God wanted him to be in terms of Christian maturity. He was to grow in Christlikeness, not simply to get by which is not growth but retardation! From eternity past God orchestrated all the events described in the book of Job. A proper understanding of the book of Job enables believers to move beyond following in Job's footsteps. As precious as Job the person was, we acknowledge that Job was not Christ. He was to become like Christ. God had Job in the school of Christian maturity as He did Jesus (Hebrews 2:10; 4:15-16; 5:7-10). Jesus, the apostles, and Job graduated but believers will remain in school as a student and teacher until Christ returns. Every believer is to be a student like Christ. When that happens men will acknowledge the fact that these believers were appointed to be *with* Christ (Mark 4:13), in order to be *like Him* (Luke 6:40;

Acts 4:13). God is glorified as the world is introduced to Christ through His people.

The goal and reality for and of every believer is to imitate Christ which is done by following in His footsteps (Matthew 10:32-38; 16:24-28; Mark 8:34-38; Luke 9:23; 14:27; John 12:25). That means the believer will change his thinking, wanting, and doing and bring them in line with biblical truth (Psalm 119:9-11). Perhaps God will provide us with more astute counselors and friends to help us change our view of God, His providence, and self. In that way, we will use both hard and easy times as a tool to become more like Christ. When that happens God is glorified and the believer reaches new heights in spiritual maturity. He has a foretaste of heaven!

It is easy to miss a simple summary of the Christian life in terms of growth as given in Romans 8:28-29 and Genesis 50:19-21 when faced with hard times. So I repeat: God, His thoughts, His desires, and His ways, must not be disguised, distorted, or hidden by a person's feelings, experience, or understanding. Biblically-based truth must not and will not be trumped by feelings; reason must not be divorced from the whole counsel of God. Bits and pieces of biblical truth served as the main course doesn't satisfy and only aggravates hunger and stifles growth. Such was the case produced by the three friends. Their counsel presented only one aspect of God and His ways. It was less than truthful and it was harmful. They spoke ill of God.

Such it is with every blatant false counsel and every counsel that emphasizes only one truth about God.

Job exposed himself to God's judgment when he questioned God's incomprehensibility. It was only when God confronted Job that the true knowledge of God and of man became evident. One of the goals of knowledge of God's incomprehensibility is to shut mouths and open hearts. The two are linked.

Application

1. A veil of mystery surrounds God. This serves at least two purposes: God is holy and man is protected. By it God woos His people to come but through a "mediator."

   a. How does that fact fit Isaiah 55:1-10 and Matthew 11:28-30?

   b. Why should anyone come to God?

   c. Why did Job come to God?

   d. What was the outcome?

   e. How do you apply Psalm 34:8 to your life? Be specific.

2. How satisfied are you with God? Be specific and give reasons.

3. What must you do to enjoy God and taste His goodness (Psalm 34:8; Philippians 3:7-11)? Give examples.

CHAPTER 22

A Comparison of Job and John the Baptist

THIS MAY SEEM TO BE a strange comparison. However, as I was reading the gospels, I was struck by what John the Baptist, the penultimate prophet, knew and did not know. In that sense he was like Job.

John the Baptist had no desire to hold on to his disciples and his position. His knowledge of Christ influenced him in his ministry. He pursued his mission of making straight the way for Christ. John continued his ministry, but his circumstances changed radically as did Job's. He had been ministering truth to everyone, but King Herod's wife took offense and Herod imprisoned him. While in prison, John sought assurance regarding his understanding of Jesus: was Jesus the Messiah (Matthew 11:2-3)?

Similarly, Job knew who he was or so he thought. He also had a ministry. He prayed for and offered sacrifices for his children. We know of only one interaction with his wife — when she offered satanic counsel. In the midst of God's hard providence, Job swiftly and respectfully counseled her (Job

2:9-10). His circumstances also radically changed, and he was functionally incapacitated and imprisoned.

Both John and Job received counsel. But unlike John, Job received misleading counsel that was laced with partial truths. Both John and Job wanted answers and reassurance as to what God was to up. John sent his disciples to Jesus and Job demanded an explanation from God.

First, consider what each knew. Job had a vibrant, healthy relationship with God. God said so (Job 1:1, 3, 8; 2:3). Job was God's man in covenant with God. Job was aware of the importance of covenantal faithfulness. Job was Holy Spirit-oriented and energized. Therefore, he ministered to others and to his family. He prayed and offered sacrifices for his children. He received counsel from his three friends that he must repent; but unlike John's message of repentance, it was to get out of a "bad" situation No mention is made of Job's personal repentance until Job 42:6.

John the Baptist also had a close relationship with God. He knew he was called by God for a specific purpose (John 1:19-29). Job had no idea that was true of himself! In response to the priests and Levites sent from Jerusalem, John confessed that he was not the Christ, Elijah, or the Prophet. As a prophet John bore a strong resemblance with Elijah. I will return to this point. Rather he was fulfilling prophecy (Exodus 23:20; Isaiah 40:3-5; Malachi 3:1). John was God's man in covenant with God.

He was a witness to and preparer of Christ's coming. He was making ready the way for *and* to the Messiah. His message was one of repentance. But in contrast to the counsel of Job's three friends, John knew Israel was a covenant breaker and as such was in grave danger. The end of Israel as a nation was imminent unless there was repentance and covenantal fruitfulness. God's judgment was near and Israel was not ready. Israel must repent if she was to avoid God's judgment.

Second, both were faced with the sovereignty, the wisdom, and the incomprehensibility of God. Both wondered what God was doing. Job ministered and took care of his family. Then his world collapsed. He lost things, people, family, and physical health. He received misguided and even ungodly counsel via his wife and semi-godly counsel from his three friends. What now? He was in the dark from his perspective not knowing how to reconcile what he knew about God and himself and his lot (Job 3). He acted upon the seeming reality of the absence of and seemingly uncaring God. He did not hear a kind or encouraging word from God. We know God eventually gave him the greatest encouragement: God brought Job to Himself and restored him.

John the Baptist also began well. He was a relative of Jesus (Luke 1:36). Jesus publicly identified Himself with John's ministry and was baptized by John (Matthew 3:13-17; Luke 3:21-22). John and Jesus had overlapping ministries. John's gospel recorded an extraordinary picture of the Baptist (1:35-42 and 3:22-30). The

Baptist was with two of his disciples. When he saw Jesus, he announced Jesus as the Lamb of God. These two men left the Baptist and followed Jesus. John knew he must decrease. Such was the case in John 3 when the question of who is number One arose based on who was winning the *baptizing* war. John gives his answer in 3:30. It was not about John but about Christ. In that sense John seemed to be farther along than Job in terms of spiritual maturity and humility.

Third, neither Job nor John knew what God was doing in the moment or what was to be the final outcome. Job wondered, lamented, complained, and even wanted to take God to court to give an account of Himself. However, the fact of God's control was never in question for Job. Rather, the question of the wisdom and goodness of that control was. For Job, God's providence — Job's situation — declared that God's wisdom and grace were non-existent or at least hidden and unavailable to him. Job could not see the end and therefore he assumed that he could did not see God and His purposes. He likened his condition to darkness and death both of which he preferred and interpreted as an escape from his troubles (Job 3). He only saw from a *now* and temporal perspective.

Before chapters 38-42, Job's frame of reference was captured by the thought: doesn't my relationship with God protect me and my family from "bad things" in this life? This was Satan's challenge to God regarding Job. Through it, Satan was attempting to bring God down. Job did not know he was part of Satan's scheme and less did he know that he was part of God's plan! Believers are not to make the same mistake!

John the Baptist did not hear Jesus' words given in Matthew 11:1-19 and Luke 7:18-35. He was in prison for being faithful. He sent his disciples to ask Jesus: Are you really the Messiah (11:2-3). John knew that judgment for unrepentant Israel was at hand. He had taught that Jesus was the Lamb of God. For his efforts he was in prison with no escape. Jesus was still alive; no change had occurred in Israel; the same church leaders were in power; there had been no change in their teachings; and he was doomed. Like Job, John wondered "what was going on." Had God made a mistake or a miscalculation?

John sent his disciples to Jesus to discover facts. Like Job, John wanted an answer. Jesus responded to the disciples of John and gave them a report to give to John. Jesus quoted the prophecy found in Isaiah 61, the text He used at His inaugural public sermon in the synagogue (Luke 4:18-22). After they left, Jesus gave a wonderful testimony about John: *I tell you the truth: Among those born of women there has not been anyone greater than John the Baptist . . .* (11:11). Unlike Job who received God's blessing in his present life, apparently John died never hearing Jesus' words about him.

Fourth, Job and John were faced with God in the circumstances He had ordained from eternity past. Both asked questions. Unlike Job, we don't know how many times that John questioned God. However, faithfulness or lack of it was the key for both. Both appeared to stumble in their faithfulness. We know Job was restored. Even though Job and John the Baptizer are not mentioned in the chapter 11 of the book of Hebrews, we know that in the end both were faithful. The chapter offers an important perspective of those who have practiced long faithfulness and long obedience in the same direction but did not see with their physical eyes what they hoped to see (*these were all commended for their faith; yet none of them received what had been promised. God had planned something better for us so that only together with us would they be made perfect*: Hebrews 11:39-40; see 1 John 1:6-7). Job, and we suspect John as well but are not told, were able to taste God's goodness. We are told that Job certainly did in this life in a profound way. In the end, all believers will taste and continue to taste God Himself!

The promise of resurrection should be a powerful motivator for pleasing God daily. Resurrection life begins at salvation and enables a person to keep an eternal perspective enabling them to be of earthly good (Romans 6:9-11; Colossians 3:1-3; 1 John 3:1-3). Resurrection life, eternal life and a foretaste of heaven begin at salvation and with a relationship (Romans 6:9-10; John 17:3). We are not told how much Job and John knew about the resurrection and resurrection life which begins at salvation (See the section: Job's knowledge of the Gospel). We know that God gives His children the necessary resources including Himself to endure God's way for His glory. Both men knew Genesis 22 and the concept of a substitutionary sacrifice. Faithful Abraham found the animal for the sacrifice as a substitute for Isaac. It pointed to resurrection life which began then. Isaac was saved and his life was spared because of the substitute (Galatians 3:6, 8)! Both were able to begin to look vertically and eternally which enabled them to walk by faith not by sight.

Both Job and John must have agreed that this world is not heaven and that heaven is a place of joyful intimacy and fellowship with the living God. These facts are strong motivators for faithful, God-pleasing living as evidenced by the saints (Hebrews 11:39-40).

There is a learning curve for the believer. Growth in Christlikeness occurs in the believer and growth in satanic likeness occurs in the unbeliever. The believer's growth comes in various forms and in various ways. We are told that Job grew (Job 40 and 42). We assume that John did as well. Knowing the specifics of the final outcome seemed important at the time. In contrast, simply knowing that God had ordained the end and the means to the end is vital for growth in Christlikeness (Colossians 3:1-3; 1 John 3:1-3). This perspective gives hope and strength. The end is God's prerogative and growth is the Christian's joy and responsibility. He is indwelt by the Holy

Spirit who does not work against or without the believer. He always works in and with the believer.

Jesus trusted the Triune God and He practiced these truths (Hebrews 12:1-3). Jesus is the grand Model of trusting and obeying for no other purpose than to glorify and to please His Father. As such He completed the work of the Triune God (John 5:19-30; 6:37-43; 10:28-30). When believers trust and obey they complete the true circle of life described in 1 John 4:7-12. God is the Fountainhead of love; He loved His people into the kingdom and in response they love others (Romans 5:6-10; 1 John 4:7-12).

Jesus always had the big picture in view (Hebrews 12:1-3). This enabled Him to run the race with endurance. Knowing the end was more important than knowing every specific step of the way. "Knowing more facts" is not the key. Feelings and experiences tempt the believer to attempt to discover what God is doing. In one sense, every believer knows what God is "up to" — gaining His glory and maturing His children which glorifies Him. In another sense, God may withhold the specifics. However, God never withholds Himself and truth. Saving faith always seeks understanding and rejoices in the quest and the gain. Understanding always seeks faithfulness and faith always seeks understanding.

Trust is not to be defective by one's lack or limited knowledge of God and the outcome in any situation. If it were, it would not be trust (Hebrews 11:1, 6)! Rather knowing that God is and that He is good and purposeful in all circumstances should motivate believers to focus on pleasing God in every situation (Romans 8:28-29). This is the ultimate Christ-like activity and is what glorifies the Father and the Son (John 17). This is what satisfies God and is what should satisfy the believer. Glorifying God is the reason God created man and is the reason for the Son coming to earth. Developing a "sight" for God's glory on earth prepares the believer for heaven. Without a taste and sight of His glory on earth, the person will never see the glorious God in heaven. Growth in Christlikeness now prepares the believer for heaven and it increases the anticipation of being there.

Jesus knew the end and that knowledge motivated Him to correctly interpret the present. He was able to please His Father all the way to and on the cross and beyond (Hebrews 12:1-3). Jesus glorified the Father every moment He was on earth. In John 17, He prayed for the fuller manifestation of that glory as He moved toward the cross. He looked forward to the cross for that purpose — glorifying the Triune God. He prayed that believers would see His glory, in part, by rightly interpreting the cross and His work the years prior to the cross and as he hung on the cross (John 17:24-26). Believers will follow in Christ footsteps as they grow in their amazement of God's glory and its significance.

Let's return to Elijah and John the Baptist and see how they fit into our picture of Job. As mentioned, John had a striking resemblance to Elijah. Many Israelites believed Elijah must come before the Messiah (Matthew 11:13-14; 17:12-13; Mark 1:2, 9-11), a conviction probably based on Malachi 3:1; 4:5. Jesus associated John with Elijah.

Who was Elijah (1 Kings 17-19; 2 Kings 2:1-2)? He appears suddenly in 1 Kings 17 and disappears fairly suddenly in 2 Kings 2. There is no record of a prophetic call or a divine oracle given or spoken to him. He was a praying man (James 5:17). He prayed fervently for a curse — a drought, as part of the covenant that bound God and Israel (Deuteronomy 11:16-17). His prayer was in response to wickedness and the royally-sanctioned idolatrous worship of Baal (1 Kings 16:31-33).

God blessed Elijah when He answered Elijah's prayer for both drought and rain. Elijah was blessed with power and energy as he demolished the prophets of Baal (1 Kings 18). Elijah challenged the people of Israel to declare loyalty to God (1 Kings 18:21) or the prophets of Baal (1 Kings 18:22-29) and indirectly Ahab and Jezebel who ascribed to and orchestrated Israel as an idolatrous nation. In this way Elijah was like Job — both had success as provided by God.

Elijah's life changed as did Job's. Again people speak of circumstances or life as if they are divorced from God. A response to God's providence is a response to God. As we have seen Job was a man of God who offered sacrifices and he was a blessing to his family and friends and who had a place of honor in the community. Elijah was a man of God who took on proud and rebellious Israel and her king (Ahab) and his wife and won a great victory for the Lord. So what was the problem with Elijah? His "fortunes" changed just as did Job's. Jezebel displayed her disdain for God by showing her disdain for Elijah (1 Kings 19:1-2). This is so reminiscent of Satan in God's presence and his attack on God through Job. Jezebel was Satan incarnate. She was after God through Elijah. If she could take out Elijah she would discredit his God and retain control over Israel.

Elijah's response was similar to Job's (19:3). Fearful he ran assuming he was running from Jezebel but he was running from God. Amazingly this man of God, who had been given great victories over the false prophets and the elements, ran from and not to God. Again this is reminiscent of Job's response.

Similarly God met Elijah. Try as he might, he could not leave God. After God fed him and rested him (19:5-9), God presented Himself to Elijah. This is similar to God's dealings with Job as recorded in Job 38-42. God asked him a question: *What are you doing here, Elijah?* (v. 9, 13). God gave him the command to stand in His presence via tangible signs of a theophany: (v. 11: the wind and the earthquake and in v. 12: the fire). But Elijah did not get it. When a fourth sign was given, a gentle whisper, a sound of sheer or pregnant silence, he still gave the same answer: I am the only one (v. 13-14).

Perhaps Elijah was looking for a repeat Sinai experience as Moses had. He did not get those signs for several reasons:

redemptive revelation had progressed — God was not merely a God who revealed Himself in natural forces; God is covenantally faithful and revealed Himself as such; and He had retained a remnant (Romans 11:2-4). Prophets were to be judged by their faithfulness in proclaiming God's teaching and demonstrating faithfulness to God. Elijah was to be a man of faithful action as well as a man of words.

Elijah answered God based on his understanding of God and his circumstances. He declared to God that he was the only one left, the only one faithful to God, and that his life was threatened (v. 10, 14). The answers suggested that Elijah believed God had missed it! Again this approach to God and His ways is reminiscent of Job's initial approach to God. Both Job and Elijah did not understand God and His ways. Specifically, Elijah did not understand the significance of God's self-revelation and he seemed to discredit it. Unlike Job who did get it finally, Elijah did not seem to get it.

Yet God was merciful to him and richly blessed him as God did Job. Both he and Job had work to do. Job interceded for his friends and Elijah was commissioned to do anoint Elisha who would anoint two kings, Hazael and Jehu (1 Kings 19:15-17). He called Elisha and subsequently Elijah was taken up into heaven God (2 Kings 2).

God is gracious to His people no matter their position and where they stand in redemptive history. Understanding is not necessarily the key. Job did not understand God's ways and demanded an explanation and eventually was willing to take God to court. Elijah did not get the point. He had functioned as God's man, a man of great zeal and action; he had earned a great victory for God through his loyalty but he discovered that sin and satanic influence were alive and well. Elijah wanted to know why: what is God up to! Elijah wondered how come he was not more successful. As Job, Elijah desired that which was not his to know. Like Moses, Elijah died outside the Promised Land before God's work was completed. Yet each were present at the Mount of Transfiguration indicating their role in redemptive history. Both Job and Elijah learned that this is God's world and He is the ruler yet (Psalm 2 and 8; Acts 4:24; 17:24-32).

Application

1. Job and John were special people set aside by God. Circumstances came that forced them to interpret and reinterpret what God was up to.

   a. What did each do?

   b. What were the results?

2. When God and His ways do not seem to make sense to you, what do you think, desire, and do? What are the results?

3. How is Romans 8:28-29 a blessing to you? Be specific.

4. We are told of Job's restoration while he was still on this earth. We assume that John the Baptist was blessed by Jesus' message to John's disciples.

   a. How is Hebrews 11:39-40 a blessing to you?

   b. How does it help you to be content with God and His ways? See Philippians 2:14-17.

5. Elijah was considered a great prophet yet he lacked something.

   a. What was it?

   b. What was God's question?

   c. Elijah was to look up and to the future. What kept him from doing that? How was he like Job?

   d. How do we know he "got" it?

CHAPTER 23

Job: A Type of Christ: Part I

Humiliation and Humility

ONE MEANS OF LINKING THE Old and New Testaments is Christologically. The statement by Augustine, "the new is in the old concealed; the old is in the new revealed" expresses the way in which the two testaments of the Bible are interrelated. The key for understanding the New Testament in its fullest is to see in it the fulfillment of those things that were revealed in a concealed or incomplete form in the Old Testament. The Old Testament points forward in time, preparing God's people for the work of Christ in the New Testament.

The Bible has at least three unifying elements: a Person, a plan, and a program. The Person is Christ. The plan is best termed redemption. Redemption is actually the fulfillment of the eternal, Intratrinitarian Covenant of Grace or Peace as described by Jesus (John 6:37-43). In eternity past, the Trinity ordained salvation for a people — God's people. The third element is the program which is summarized in Kingdom and covenantal language — Israel in the Old Testament and the New Israel, the

Church, in the New Testament. God saved individually and corporately. (I am indebted to Dr. Sidney Dyer, professor of Greek and New Testament at Greenville Theological Seminary and his class entitled *The Gospels and Acts* for this overview).

The prophets including John the Baptist, the penultimate prophet, announced the coming and nature of the Kingdom of God and the requirements for entering it (John 3:3-8). Jesus Christ, the final Prophet and King, redeems His people through His kingdom program. Behind the Son's redemptive work is the agreement made in eternity past in which the Father gave His Son a people, the Son agreed to redeem them, and the Holy Spirit agreed to apply the Son's redemptive work to God's people (John 6:37-43). The Triune God did not and will not lose any of His people (John 10:12-18, 28-29). This includes Job! There is unity between the Old and New Testaments because there is unity within the Trinity. The redemptive message and program are the same.

The book of Job is of special importance in explaining God's redemptive program. The opening chapters of the book of Job take us back to the Garden of Eden (Genesis 3). In the Garden, satanic counsel was aimed at reversing the Creator-creation distinction. Both Adam and Job were called by God and placed in their circumstances for a reason. The book of Job opens with a statement about Job. In Job 1:5 we are told that as head of the family, Job was a priest for God and a type of the first Adam. He interceded for his children. In that sense he was a type of Christ

(Romans 8:34; Hebrews 7:25). He feared that his children might curse God in their hearts. This was the sin that Satan predicted Job would commit (1:11; 2:5) and the sin that Job's wife suggested he commit (2:9).

Satan predicted God's failure through and by Job's presumed fall. God set the stage quite dramatically declaring that Job was Christ-like (1:1, 8; 2:3). God "set up" Satan! Satan took the first Adam to task in the Garden and attempted to take Christ to task throughout His ministry beginning in the wilderness at the inauguration of Christ's Messianic ministry (Matthew 4 and Luke 4). It "worked" in the Garden, so why not in the wilderness and why not with Job?

Job held a place of honor in general and among his family. He was a provider, an intercessor, and a deliverer. And like Christ, initially, he was respected and blessed in his position. However, as we have seen, in God's providence, God brought Job low. God placed him in a state of humiliation. Please note, that in the book that bears his name, Job was not a humble man until the end. In contrast, Jesus freely placed Himself in a state of humiliation as a humble man. He continued to humble Himself throughout His life on earth all the way to the cross. He is the Model for humility.

As I have discussed, humiliation and humility are often equated which is incorrect. Rather humiliation refers to some experience or life event that is considered shameful and degrading depending on one's standard. That definition misses the point of God's sovereignty. No event or situation just happens. Mankind is a responder so every person responds in some manner to his circumstances and thus to God. Humiliation is that which is outside of a person.

On the other hand, humility is a whole-person response by the person in his situation. It is a response by a person to God and to others. Thus it has both a vertical and horizontal reference. It is a reflection of and demonstration of one's heart. Humility is an honest esteeming of oneself as small in as much as a person is. It is an inner-man activity of evaluation and judgment. It is an estimate of oneself based on a standard. For the believer, humility is the correct estimate of himself based on God's standard especially before God (Philippians 2:3-5). The humble person rightly knows himself, others, and God and responds accordingly. Humbling oneself requires God's grace, both saving grace and sanctifying grace. Situations — humiliations — don't humble a person. They are the context in which a person humbles himself or boasts in himself rather than in Christ (Galatians 6:14; James 4:6-10; 1 Peter 5:6).

Jesus voluntarily humbled Himself the moment He left heaven and entered into an estate of humiliation. His focus was on glorifying God, pleasing the Father, and covenantal faithfulness. Jesus is the example par excellence of humility. Proper knowledge is one key to developing humility. Another key is relational. Jesus knew Himself, the Triune God, and others perfectly. Moreover, He knew the mind of God and the reason that He had come as the Godman. He chose to hide His glory and God-ness (Philippians 2:5-8). Amazing!

The fact that the glory of God was hidden is in itself simply mind-boggling. The fact that Christ saves a people through humbling Himself all the way to cross and beyond is even more stupendous. Moreover, as equally stupendous, is the fact that fallen man, arrogant, ignorant, and rebellious, does not perish before Christ, but is transformed into a child of God by the work of the Holy Spirit.

Unlike Christ, Job did not volunteer for his state of humiliation. He was placed in very unpleasant, humiliating conditions. He did not place himself there. In this way, his kingship was removed, and he was considered a trouble-deserving sinner by his friends. He was stripped of his possessions, family, friends, and health, all that was dear to him. He understood that he was in his situation because of God's power and control.

We observed that Job clung to his assertion that he was innocent and therefore did not deserve God's hard providence. In other words, Job did not think he deserved to be treated by God — he never denied sovereignty — the way he was being treated. He wanted to be treated better than the Father treated Jesus! Initially he seemed "content" to voice these complaints. As he remained in his situation, he began to demand to speak with God and present to Him his case for "acquittal." He expected vindication and God to give it to him and or explain Himself.

In that sense, I believe Job rebelled. Many may think that is too strong an assertion. But the fact remains Job did not humble himself. As a result, he lived the lie.

Job wanted to take God to court and have Him explain Himself. Often believers function in the same God-dishonoring manner. God expects us to learn from Job. If Job was here today, I suspect he would tell believers that he was not God and that he grieves that he believed and functioned as if he was. He would say the God-given situation was extremely disconcerting but a gift. Job humbly called out to God because he stopped competing and dishonoring God.

Application

1. The redemptive story runs throughout Scripture. Connect the unity of the Old and New Testament in terms of God's plan, person, and program. Begin with eternity, move to Genesis 1-2 then to Genesis 3:15, through the Old Testament, into the gospels, the epistles, and end with Revelation 22:17-21.

   a. What do you learn?

   b. How would this knowledge have been a blessing to Job?

2. What is the difference between humiliation and humility?

3. Job longed for what and why?

4. What was God's answer?

CHAPTER 24

Job: A Type of Christ: Part II

The Cross

THEOLOGICALLY WE SPEAK OF JESUS' estate of or state of humiliation. Often we think of that word as being inclusive of His circumstances and His response. But we must be careful here. One way to be careful is to recognize the difference between humiliation (the situation) and humility (a whole-person response of the person in the circumstances). Humiliation refers to situations, people, and circumstances that are grouped under God's providences. They come to pass because God ordained them. However and against the common "wisdom" of the day, circumstances don't change a person. They are the context in which the person demonstrates his theology and the significance of his relationship with God in Christ by the Holy Spirit. It also demonstrates the significance of God's relationship to the person in his situation. Humility as I have mentioned earlier, is the result or product of the person's response to his circumstances. In His estate of humiliation, Jesus humbled Himself. However a person may be humiliated but sinfully respond to God and His providence with anger, bitterness, resentfulness, grumbling, and or complaining. Sadly, the believer too often uses the situation — God's providence — as an excuse for sinning.

By the Triune God's providence, Jesus was brought low — He left heaven. He brought Himself low. He lowered Himself from His privileged position according to the eternal plan of the Triune God (John 6:37-43). Functionally the Trinity was separated, but by design. It was done in order to accomplish redemption. If there had been no humiliation and no humility, there would be no redemption. The three are linked.

Jesus came to earth, took a body to His deity; He was born, lived under the law, and was subject to the wrath and condemnation that comes from lawbreaking. Yet He was not a sinner or lawbreaker! He was the Lawgiver and Lawkeeper. He had no guilt from His own sin and from Adam's sin and God's judgment of Adam's first sin. Yet He became what He was not. He was humiliated. His humiliation began long before the cross. Leaving heaven and taking on humanity began His humiliation. It reached its pinnacle at the cross.

The above sentences attempt to describe Jesus' humiliation — what occurred outside of Him. They don't describe His humility. Jesus humbled Himself as the Godman in the context of His humiliation (Matthew 11:28-30; Philippians 2:5-8; 2 Corinthians 5:21; 8:9; Hebrews 4:15-16; 5:7-10). The scenario seems so strangely amazing because it is! It gives the believer a perspective on God (Romans 3:21-26; 5:6-10). The Triune God opens Himself to the world in a way that the world cannot and will not understand until and unless they are regenerated — that is they undergo a heart change by the Holy Spirit.

As part of humbling Himself, Jesus made a perfect assessment of Himself in light of John 6:37-43 with the motivation to glorify God and to please His Father (John 4:31-34). Jesus, the second person of the Trinity and God's Son, was humiliated. Moreover, He humiliated Himself! But the events and circumstances did not humble Him. They are the context in which a person demonstrates his theology by his response. I repeat: Jesus humbled Himself prior to His coming and in the context of His God-ordained circumstances — His providence. Unless He had humbled Himself, He would not have come!

He placed Himself in those circumstances with the proper motivation — to please His Father. He remained faithful because He desired to please and glorify His Father more than He desired to please Himself. The two are inexorably linked.

Even more astounding is the fact that by pleasing His Father He was pleasing Himself. Therefore, He prayed that he would be glorified as the Father was glorified (John 17:1-5, 24-26). The two are linked! He was not seeking pleasure per se, otherwise He would be using God. Yet He obtained God's pleasure and His own pleasure as He lived as the True Son. He longed for the Triune God to be glorified and He knew His ministry was vital to achieving that goal. His program for life on earth as the Messiah was the eternal plan of God and His motivation was to please and glorify His Father. Pleasing and being pleased were linked and occurred and will occur through the twin pillars of humiliation and humility.

Job was placed in a position of disgrace and humiliation. Job had no inkling that God works through, in, and by hard providences — the presence of evil. Unlike Christ, Job did not volunteer for it or enter into it graciously. But like Christ he was stripped of that which was important and dear to him. However, contrary to Satan's logic, possessing material and physical things and health were not the true issues for Job. Job was concerned about his relationship with God — was it intact and secure?

One fundamental fact was clear. God did not divorce Jesus or Job. Even on the cross, when Jesus as the Godman cried out as to why the Father had forsaken Him, He knew the answer (Matthew 27:46; Mark 15:34). The Godman was forsaken but not Christ, the second person of the Triune God. Jesus Christ, the Messiah and Godman had to be forsaken according to the Triune God's eternal plan.

Christ's humility far exceeded the magnitude of His humiliation. I repeat, humbling Himself was motivated by the desire to glorify the Triune God and to please His Father. He grew as the humble Servant of God in order to accomplish His Messianic mission (Hebrews 4:15-16; 5:7-10; John 17:1-5, 24-26).

The book of Job bears testimony to Job's changed position. He fell from a place of honor and dignity. He was despised, ridiculed, and made to be a laughingstock (Job 6:1-4, 8-10, 14-16, 25-27; 7:2-4, 7-11, 16-21; 10:3, 17;12:46; 13:4-5, 28; 14:2-6; 24:7, 10 — see 22:6). Job held on to a prerogative that he thought was his on the basis of his relationship with God. He reasoned that God owed him an explanation. Until Job 38-42, Job had not humbled himself in spite of the fact that he was in deep trouble. It is one thing to acknowledge rights. It is another thing to demand them.

As a child of God, every child is privileged and entitled to all the rights and privileges of membership in God's family and kingdom (the theological term for this is adoption). Those rights were earned by Christ's perfect lawkeeping and cross-bearing and gifted to every one of His brothers and sisters. Every child of God has the right and privilege to inquire of God and even to expect Him to be faithful. But no one has the right to demand of God anything. Jesus never made demands on the Father or the Holy Spirit.

In the book of Job, no one mentioned in chapters 3-37 understood the glory of the cross. The three friends believed and acted on their belief that bad things happen only to bad people. For them, the cross would prove that Jesus was a bad person (Isaiah 53:4). They could not understand and would not accept the truth that Christ did not live and die for "good" people. He died only for impotent, rebellious, enemies, and sinners (Romans 5:6-10). He lived and died for them in spite of themselves with an agenda for them to change.

It was not until Job 38-42 that Job began to develop a proper view of the cross. It was a theological must, a redemptive necessity, for Christ to humble Himself not simply to be humiliated. Moreover, Christ must have humbled Himself all the way to the cross as well as stand trial and stay on the cross if God was to save a people and glorify Himself. Moreover, a crucified Godman was necessary for redemption, but He must be a glorified One. That occurred at the resurrection!

These facts should be amazingly and joyfully humbling! Christ's humiliation was the context in which Christ humbled Himself. It was essential that Jesus step into that humiliation and grow in humility (Hebrews 2:10; 4:15-16; 5:7-10). Eventually Job did humble himself. That became evident as he repented which is one feature of humility. Proud people don't repent (James 4:6-10; 1 Peter 5:5-7). The three friends' view of God and themselves made it impossible for them to grasp the fact that Jesus Christ was no sinner even though He was treated as one. That latter truth is part of the wisdom of the cross. It is counterintuitive and countercultural (1 Corinthians 1:18-31). The sadness of the three friends and their false theology is their misunderstanding and perhaps rejection of the cross.

The glory and the way of the cross is *down* before one goes *up*. One must descend in order for him to ascend (John

12:23-29; 1 Corinthians 1:18-31). In Job's case, Job was placed in humiliating circumstances, but initially he did not humble himself. After his meeting with God, he marvelously and spectacularly acknowledged himself for who he was and God for who He was (Job 42:5-6). He then correctly brought together the vertical and horizontal. Repentance was a fruit and a sign of increasing humility. Unlike believing sinners, Jesus humbled Himself, but He did not repent. There was no need! He was the sinless, holy, blameless, and pure Lamb of God (2 Corinthians 5:21; Hebrews 7:26).

Ezekiel conveys this same thought regarding humility and repentance — the people of Israel will *loathe* themselves for the patterned evil that they had done and then, and only then, will they know God (Ezekiel 6:8-10; 20:43; 36:31). The word translated as loathe carries the idea of considering yourself nauseating putrefaction as did Job's words recorded in Job 42:6 In Israel's and Job's cases it was the only response to a proper self-judgment.

Please notice that the correct knowledge of God always leads to a correct knowledge of self and vice versa. Thankfully for God's people, Jesus humbled Himself by leaving heaven and functionally the Godhead for a time. He stepped into humiliating circumstances being born in a dirty place — stable or cave. The dirty and stinky surroundings represented the heart of the people.

Job did not agree to take a *fall* for mankind. In his situation, he demanded an accounting from God. He was a type of Christ in that he "fell" from a place of distinction and entered a sin-cursed world with faulty friends and wife, loss of physical things, loss of health, and the drudgery of the slow passage of time. However, although he clung to God's relationship with him, he was not a model of Christ and humility until the end. In contrast, Christ clung to His relationship with the Triune God throughout His life all the way to the cross and beyond (John 10:30). He voluntarily stepped out of heaven into humiliating circumstances because of His love of the Father and His desire to glorify and please Him. It is worth repeating, Jesus' goal was to accomplish the eternal plan of the Godhead (John 6:37-43). Jesus was pleased to be able to glorify and to please His Father even if and especially if the cross was the means for doing so. Praise God!

Application

1. There is unity between the Old and New Testaments. Job was a reluctant player in God's providential plan. But he grew and was excited and overjoyed that he had entered into the presence of God.

   a. Where are you in your view of God's power, control, and goodness?

   b. Do you strive to see the eternal purpose?

    c. If so how?

    d. How do you apply Romans 8:28-29 to every situation in your life?

2. What did Job learn?

3. Job missed the big point as many of us do. Keeping God's redemptive plan in view should motivate you to please God out of blessing, privilege, and duty.

    a. Summarize God's redemptive plan.

    b. Give examples in your own life how recalling the plan enabled you to get victory in your situation.

CHAPTER 25

Job and Peter

Luke 22:31-34

LUKE, THE PHYSICIAN, GIVES INSIGHT into Jesus Christ, the sympathetic High Priest and Savior of people from all nations, Jew and Gentile. Jesus was and is the Godman, truly God and truly man, one person and two natures. Luke emphasized His humanity. Those facts help set the stage for Jesus' encounter with Peter and all the apostles given in Luke 22:31-34. The group was dining at the last Supper. Christ taught kingdom presence and conferred membership in it on the eleven apostles (22:29-30). In the next verse, Jesus told Peter and the group that Satan asked for Jesus' permission to sift them — all of the apostles (v. 31). The word translated *ask* in the original language means to beg something of someone, and it is used only here in New Testament. The word does not mean to obtain by simply asking. Satan's request takes us back into the heavenlies as documented in Job 1-2. Satan is not in control. As God's agent, he must have permission for his activity especially when directed at God's people. He will never be in control. He is not a free spirit but a created being who marches to God's design.

Consider that at this hour of His earthly life, Jesus is confidently proclaiming His sovereign control. Jesus is the Victor even when it appears He is not! This truth is highlighted by the simple fact that Satan requested, not demanded, to sift all the disciples. We are not told when or how this request was made. The word in the original language translated as *sift* means to shake in order to separate, inspect, or sort. It carries the idea of winnow and is used only here in the New Testament. The "you" is plural in verse 31 and it is singular in verse 32.

Jesus frequently taught in the milieu. Jesus desired that all the apostles and especially Peter would comprehend that the temptation of covenantal unfaithfulness a constant, 24/7 reality and fact of life. The temptation comes in the form of choosing to please God (covenantal faithfulness) or to please self. Jesus faced this same fact throughout His life. It was more marked (if that is possible!) after His time in the wilderness (Matthew 4 and Luke 4) and as the cross drew near. The temptation was part of His humiliation. He had a choice. By it, He, the second person of the Trinity, was put in the position of choosing to forsake the eternal Intratrinitarian harmony and unity. Jesus placed Himself in this position and was victorious as evidenced by consistently choosing to glorify and please God. Self-glorification and self-pleasing came by way of covenantal faithfulness (Hebrews 12:1-3)! Simply, He went to and left the cross as the Victor!

In Job 1-2, the Holy Spirit gave the reader a glimpse into how God works in His world and for His people. In both Job and in Luke, the Triune God had Job, Peter, and the apostles in His grasp (John 10:28-30). However, at those moments described in Job and in Luke, none of the fore mentioned people acted on the truth that God had them. Job charged God (though he did not curse Him) and all the apostles deserted Jesus after claiming loyalty (Matthew 26:33-35; Mark 13:30-31; John 13:37).

Jesus' statement to the apostles is another testimony to the fact that Jesus was in charge during His entire lifetime. His ministry did not begin or end at the cross. In the end, Job and the apostles were people of "little faith," but they did not desert God completely or finally because God did not desert them (see John 6:37-43; 10:28-30). God loses none of His sheep (John 10:14-18, 25-27). He restores them and in this case, God sent out Job and the apostles for ministry. The perseverance of the saints is due to God's perseverance which is predicated on His trustworthiness and covenantal faithfulness. He is the covenantmaking and covenantkeeping God Who is always at work for His glory, the glory of the Triune God, and the good of His people.

Jesus said He prayed for Peter — you is singular (v. 32). Jesus gave the subject of His prayer: Peter was to be proved faithful and a blessing to others. Eventually he was but in the moment, Peter, as did all the apostles, denied and deserted Jesus. Does that fact mean that Jesus failed? Did the Triune God fail because Job "got-on-God's case"? Did Satan win? No to all three questions! Christ, the great High Priest, interceded for His people while on earth and intercedes for them in His heavenly session (Romans 8:34; Hebrews 7:25). Jesus did not and does not fail!

Job repented after he was in the presence of the living God as God's kind of student (Job 38-42). Peter wept when confronted simply by the gaze of Christ (Luke 22:60-62) and by sound — he heard the rooster's voice (Matthew 26:75; Mark 14:73; Luke 22:60-62). Jesus' ministry continued through the apostles. He restored Peter (John 21:15-19). He did not leave Peter or the other apostles even though for the moment they left Him.

Typically, and supernaturally both Job and Peter were reinstated (Job 40:2-5; 42:6; John 21). We are not told specifically that Peter repented but his weeping was not crocodile tears and it was not without hope as were Judas' tears (Matthew 27:3-5; 2 Corinthians 7:9-10). Job's assumed tears flowed from repentance and then moved to joy when he was in God's presence (Job 38-42). His heart and his senses were in sync (inner- and outer-man harmony!) and he was opened to truth. So, too, were Peter's tears which were tears of joy and understanding as he prepared for ministry to the Jews. The fullness of that understanding came at Pentecost.

Go back to the opening two chapters of the book of Job. Satan wanted to sift Job. He wanted to separate him from God. He wanted to break the relationship between God and Job thus demonstrating that God, not Job, could not be trusted. Those opening chapters demonstrate that Satan was after God through Job just as he was after God through Christ! Satan reasoned that if enough pressure was applied to Job, Job would curse God and depart from Him thus showing that God can't be trusted to keep His people (John 10:28-30; 1 Peter 1:3-5). Satan tacitly contended that no matter what God does for His people His grip is not strong enough to handle humiliation. Satan had suggested that God bought Job. Satan arrogantly challenged God!

Here in Luke we find the same scenario. Satan had not learned his lesson. Satan wanted to sift and thus separate Peter and all the apostles from the Triune God. Satan was attempting to defame God through the failure of God's children. I repeat, one of the chief messages of Scripture as emphasized by Job and Peter is the simple but profound fact that relationships matter. This fact is highlighted by and flows from the Trinity. God would no more leave or forsake His children than He would divide Himself in His very being! The Father forsook the Godman once and for all!

One may rightfully ask if one of Satan's desires is to constantly sift God's people. The Bible warns God's people to be aware. Satanic influence is outside the believer and it remains within the believer because of his previous membership in Satan's kingdom and family and remaining sinfulness of the believer. Self, always for the unbeliever and often for the believer, is at the center of fallen man's loyalty and allegiance. The pull to please self will always be evident in the believer until Jesus returns. This fact is especially true when a person is faced with unpleasantness as part of God's providence. Unpleasantness will continue until Christ returns or until the believer is called home. Until then the believer must remember and act upon the fact that the Triune God values His people because He values Himself, the Son's Messianic work, and the Holy Spirit's indwelling presence and activity. The value is not intrinsic to the believer but derived from union with Christ (1 Corinthians 1:30). It rests on what the believer is in Christ by the indwelling of the Holy Spirit and His activity (Romans 8:9; Galatians 2:20; Ephesians 3:17). This is true for believers in the Old and New Testaments!

Further, God will not leave His people because He forsook His Son once-for-all. For God to forsake His people would insult Christ and the cross and the indwelling Holy Spirit. It would break Intratrinitarian harmony and unity. The Triune God values His relationship with His people because He highly values Intratrinitarian honor, unity, and harmony. Moreover, He loves His people who are new creatures in Christ (2 Corinthians 5:17; Galatians 2:20). God did not die for good people or those with intrinsic worth (Romans 5:6-10). Believers have no intrinsic worth in and of themselves, yet they are image bearers of God which gives all men a certain dependent and special but non-salvific status before God (Psalm 8). This status is a reflection of the glory of the Creator. The believer has a "piece" of the Triune God such that he is God's and God is His. Amazing and humbling!

God extends His care — common grace — to even His enemies (Matthew 5:43-48; Acts 14:17). Fallen man has nothing within to "lure" or draw the Holy Spirit to him. On the contrary, God saves in spite of the person simply because God saves (Romans 5:6-10). This fact is captured by Jesus in John 6:44, 65 and 12:32. The term for *draw* indicates the supernatural, inside-out influence of the Holy Spirit who regenerates the believer (Romans 8:7; Titus 3:5). It is not an "against-your will" influence but a heart-opening, eye-opening, ear-opening activity that moves the now-believer to desire and seek Life and Light — Jesus Christ. In Christ by the Holy Spirit, the believer is something — he is more than simply God's image bearer. He is God's child, bought with a price, and indwelt with and by the Holy Spirit. In that sense he is something because something was done to him and in him (1 Corinthians 1:30-31; Galatians 2:20). As a result, Jesus gave Job and Peter, and all believers, the command to minister in His name. Believers are to follow suit. The magnitude and awesomeness of God's redemptive work can't be overemphasized. You, too, will persevere and minister because God has you! Job came to understand that fact and the book of Acts testifies to the apostles' rejoicing in that fact.

Application

1. What is your assessment of the similarities between Job and Peter?

2. How does the knowledge of each man strengthen and encourage you?

3. What do you learn about the Triune God from the Job-Peter comparison?

4. Have you been tempted to move away from God?

   a. Record the circumstances and your response.

   b. What truths did you rely on and what were the results?

   c. What have you done? How have you followed in Job's footsteps (Job 38-42)?

CHAPTER 26

Job: The Ultimate Lesson: God is God, Man is Not

Homework Assignment

JOB, THE BOOK AND THE man, is well-known even in the public arena. However, the main character of the book is the Triune God. The book focuses on relationships: God, Satan, and heavenly beings; God, Job, and the friends, and Job and the friends. The book highlights and focuses on the "facts of life" from several vantage points: one: covenant relationships with promises, and trustworthiness; two: God, His character, His relational activity with His people, and His purpose as Master and Controller; three: Job as a type of "every man" as student, preserver, doubter, demander, and lawyer in the context of God's providence; four: Job as a type of Christ pointing believers to a fuller and proper understanding of the cross; five: the book is not simply about getting saved. It addresses life after salvation in the midst of God's hard providence; sixth: the book helps people interpret and respond to life situations through the grid of God and His Word rather than through circumstance (hard or easy), experience, understanding divorced from God's truth, and feelings.

I. Job 1-2: a conversation with God and Satan as the angels observe:

    A. What is God's opinion of Job? 1:1,3, 8; 2:3. Answer: Job was a type of Christ and pictured in Psalm 1:1-3.

    B. What is Satan's opinion of God and of Job? 1:6-8; 2:1-2 and 1:9-11; 2:4-5: Answer: God buys people such that he is a fraud, liar, and manipulator.

    C. What was God's view of Satan? 1:12; 2:3: Answer: he is a created, rational being in God's service.

        1. He is God's instrument.

        2. See 2 Samuel 24:1 and 1 Chronicles 21:1.

        3. See Cyrus: Isaiah 41:2; 44:28-45:13; Nebuchadnezzar: Jeremiah 25:9, 27:6, 43:10

    D. What is Job's initial response to his situation in 1:20-22 and 2:10? Answer: Job held to and trusted a sovereign God who is Owner, who gives and takes away, and who is "probably" good. Early on and throughout, Job and the three friends emphasized God's power and justice.

    E. What was his wife's counsel (2:9) and whose counsel does it follow? Answer: Her only recorded words were: Curse God. It was satanic-like.

    F. What was the three friend's response to Job initially and was it helpful? See 2:11-13. Answer: Their silence must have been deafening but it was a ministry of presence. Job knew by their presence that his friends had not deserted him. In the end he wished that had!

II. Job 3-31: The three friends and their interaction with Job: The subject is God and His relationship with individuals.

A. What do you learn about the three friends (Eliphaz, Bildad, and Zophar)? Answer: They were silent but when they spoke; they misinterpreted God and Job and they gave false counsel based on reductionistic theology.

B. What is the basis for their statements to Job?

1. Job's sins have found him out — caused the trouble. Bad things happen to bad people who need to repent. Bad things don't happen to good people — look at us — so we don't need to repent. See Luke 13:1-5 and John 9:1-3.

2. Each friend's source of truth was:

a. Eliphaz: 4:12-21: feelings, experience, dreams, and mystical experience: 4-5, 15, 22

b. Bildad: 8:10-22: tradition — former generations and traditional wisdom: 8, 18, 25

c. Zophar: 11:1-20: human understanding and his own understanding of God: 11, 20

3. How would the three friends explain the cross? Answer: I suspect that would say that God metes out

tit for tat because He is righteous and just. Therefore, bad things happen to bad people. You sow what reap.

4. What would they have said to Christ at the cross? See Isaiah 53:1-12. Answer: They would have said that Jesus was getting what He deserved, and it seemed that He could even repent. Repentance would change His status.

C. What is Job's initial response as witnessed by his friends? 3:1-26: Answer: He lamented the day of his birth and his existence outside the womb. He was completely removed from God's blessings and dumbfounded. God was not blessing him, and he did not know why.

D. What is his later response to them and to God and why? Job 40 and 42. Answer: He told them they were miserable counselors, wicked, and his enemies (12:2, 4, 13:1-12; 13:1-12; 16:2; 27:7). Job will be comforted but not by the three friends (42:11). Rather he intercedes for them.

E. What did Job know or at least believe?

1. Job knew his relationship with God was right (he agreed with God initially).

2. According to traditional theology, his circumstances confirmed that his relationship with God was wrong — he was in jeopardy. How did he respond? Answer: He said whoa! He did not con-

tend that he was sinless even though the friends said he did (7:21; 13:26; 15:14-15). Job did not understand how God could be treating him this way — unjustly, warlike fashion, as his enemy when as far as he knew his relationship with God and God with him was intact. It was an expression of God's abuse of His power (13:24; 19:8-11; 24:1-12; 30:29; 33:10-11).

F. What thoughts did Job have regarding the presence of God? See 3:26; 23:2; 33:7 (see Genesis 3:8-14) — the word describing God's presence is *kabod* (others include 3:20-26; 13:27; 14:16). Answer: God's presence was a burden.

1. Compare with Psalms 32:4; 38:4.

2. What drove Job to his conclusion? Answer: His understanding of God and himself in the context of hard providence — circumstance is as follows: hard times mean you have failed, and God gets people like that. He thought relationships matter such that these hard times would not come. If they did, it indicated relational problems.

3. Was he correct? No, see chapter 1-2 and 38-42

4. How does Job's response compare with Moses' request given in Exodus 33:15-20? Answer: Boldly, both were focused on God and both wanted to be in God's presence but for different reasons.

G. Job's response:

1. What did Job demand initially? 9:28-35; 10:1-7, 8-17; 13:20-28: Answer: He wanted God to explain His actions and he wanted to argue his case with God.

2. Job still holds himself to be what? 9:26-28: Answer: He is innocent, and he wants and deserves vindication. At least he sought God. He wanted God to give him an explanation and later Job demanded God to explain Himself.

3. His circumstances implied what? 9:28-29: Answer: According to the present-day theology, Job must be a "real bad sinner."

4. He believes that the all-powerful God has not treated him with what? 10:15-16: Answer: Job holds to his innocence while God is on his case, unjust, and at enmity with Job and Job has no reason why (13:24; 19:8-11; 24:1-12; 30:29; 33:10-11).

5. Job never denies God's what? 12:7-12: Answer: He does not deny God's power and control: He does what He pleases. In 12:13-25, Job refers to God's sovereignty. But in contrast to Eliphaz (5:10-16), Job contends that God uses His power in ways that don't make sense. Job's case is one example.

6. What did Job get? See Job 38-42: Answer: He gets God because God gets him!

III. Job 32-37: Elihu's four speeches

    A. In chapters 32-33, he rebukes Job and the three friends.

        1. Elihu's speeches are a forerunner to God's rebuke of Job (33:5-10).

        2. However, his theology is reminiscence of the three friends.

        3. He is verbose, repetitious, and "full of himself."

        4. Why would God use Elihu given his theology and manner? Answer: Some believe he "prepared" the way for God's coming. The same question can be asked of God's use of the three friends. Elihu is the only counselor who referred to the Holy Spirit (32:8; 33:4), addresses Job by name (33:1, 31; 37:40) and rebukes Job for his perception of God as his enemy (33:10, 12 and 13:24 and 19:11). God agrees and in the end Job agrees: God has never been his enemy. Ignorance is not standard for judging God.

        5. Chastening is to be beneficial for the believer (33:29-30 — Roman 5:1-5; James 1:2-4; 1 Peter 1:6-7; Hebrews 12:5-11).

            1. What is chastening?

            2. How is it beneficial?

            3. Did God discipline Job?

    B. In chapter 34, Elihu asserts God's justice: 34:10.

        1. Compare 34:10 with 9:24 (14-35); 10:3; 12:4-6; 24:1-12: Job did what to God? Answer: Initially, Job charged

God with wrongdoing (Job discredited God's justice), Job said that he was God's enemy, and that God had forsaken him). Later, Job demanded a "courtroom" appearance with God. In essence, Job "bad-mouthed" God. Elihu upholds God's integrity.

2. Review Job's statement in 9:2-26:

   a. What has he concluded about God? Answer: God is a puzzle. He can't figure God out! He wonders if God is real!! He questioned God's justice.

   b. What is the basis for his conclusions? Answer: He made these conclusions based on his interpretation of God through his circumstances, feelings, and understanding. He understood that God was nowhere and if He was anywhere, He was unconcerned.

   c. How does it compare to that given in 34:10? Answer: Elihu holds fast to God's perfect justice and dealings with His people. God does as He pleases for His glory.

C. In chapters 35-37, he asserts God's goodness, power, and majesty: on what basis?

   1. 35:9-16: Answer: Men cry out for mercy rather than trusting God's justice. God hears and answers such that He is trustworthy. Elihu is the only counselor who refers to God's wisdom and joy (v.10-11). The

arrogance of the wicked is the only reason why God does not answer (v.12). It is arrogance to cry out against God's justice and silence. However, what Elihu does not add must be understood: in the throes of hard providences, God's people tend to jettison trust in God and thus lose the peace that transcends all human understanding. Thankfully, amazingly, and majestically, Jesus did not do that! Job was a type of Christ, but he was not Him.

2. 36:5-9: Answer: verses 6-9 are classic statements regarding God: He rewards the righteous and punishes sinners. However, all the counselors believed these truths were obvious in the physical, seen world. God uses His control and power to right all wrongs, punish evildoers, and to bless the righteous. Although Elihu's theology was shortsighted and reductionistic, he was combating Job's charge against God that God does not hear, let alone care (31:35-37). Neither Job nor Elihu had a correct view of God.

3. 37:5-10, 14-18, 24: Answer: God is at work and His work in creation is a testimony to God's presence, activity, and greatness. Yet He is beyond human understanding. His ways and thoughts are qualitatively and quantitatively different from

man's and they are higher than the heavens (36:26; Isaiah 55:8-9; Psalm 145:3). Elihu is highlighting the Creator-creature distinction and God's perfection in knowledge and wisdom. Elihu anticipates the divine discourses in Job 38-41 as he challenges Job to consider God's wisdom and power as the creature and not the Creator. As a result, man is to fear God (1:1,3, 8; 28;28). Interestingly God labeled Job as a man who feared God! Job had work to do!

IV. Job 38-42: God's sessions with Job and Job's response

    A. What did Job learn about God, himself, and his situation? Answer: It was rather simple: God is God and the Creator and Controller, and he is not. Job's words were few as he "soaked" in God and His truth.

    B. What was the essence of God's sessions with Job in 38-41? Answer: God took Job to creation and even to the zoo. A tsunami of truth was coming forth from God by God and Job must be ready — Job was silenced for the correct reason (Psalm 34:8; Philippians 3:7-11). Job could not get enough of God.

    C. How did he respond? 40:3-5; 42:2-6. How does his response compare with Isaiah's (Isaiah 6) and yours? Answer: He continued to humble himself which came in stages. Dramatically and progressively, Job bowed his whole person to God.

D. Job did not doubt God's sovereign control and he did not ask for healing: what are your thoughts on those facts? One Answer: God has a priority. Inner-man health leads to outer-man improvement although in varying degrees.

E. What did Job ultimately learn and do: See 42:5-6? Why? Answer: God does as He pleases which is best for everyone including God. Contrary to what some may say, Job humbled himself all the way to repentance. He confessed his arrogance and ignorance. God accepted Job.

F. What did Job do before he repented: Job 40:4-5? Answer: He was continuing to be humbled and to humble himself. He was getting the point: God is God and that is best for him and the whole world.

G. Job repentance?

1. Job 42:5-6: *I despise myself* and then he repented (5:17; 7:16; 9:21; 36:6); Luke 15:17-19: what do you think of his self-counsel? Answer: Perceiving God correctly leads to a proper self-evaluation. If you know God, you know yourself and vice versa.

2. Job 42:6 vs. 10:1: *I loathe my life* (Ezekiel 6:9; 20:43; 36:31; Psalm 119:158; 139:21). Answer: Confession and repentance is not about a "bad" self-image. Rather it focuses on a proper self-evaluation using the

word of God as the mirror into the heart. Job was something in Christ but apart from reliance on biblical truth, he is in his own world competing with God and losing but often denied.

3. Did he consider his repentance a burden or blessing? Answer: It was a blessing and a privilege for him and others.

4. The repentance was a sign of what? Answer: It was a sign that he got it — God is God and he is not. Humbling himself was the most God-pleasing activity that he could do.

H. How was this response different from the one prior to God's session with him? Answer: He spoke as the one with wisdom and control.

I. How did God respond? Answer: God blessed Job first with Himself. Job began humbling himself that culminated in repentance. God blessed others through Job and eventually he blessed Job.

V. Job was a type of Christ: See parallels with Joseph (Genesis 37-50).

A. In what ways was Job a type of Christ? Answer: Briefly, Job, Joseph, and Jesus were in a high, favored, prosperous, and exalted position. All "left" their positions. All left by God's design and His providence: Jesus through voluntary condescension and Job and Joseph by no direct sin of their own. All three would be exalted. All three faced the reality of sin's effect on them, others, and the world. All were victors because God is the Victor in Christ by the Holy Spirit (Romans 8:35-37).

B. The three friends were a type of whom? Genesis 3:1-6; Matthew 16:21-23; Answer: They gave incomplete and wrong counsel but as the truth. In that way, they followed satanic counsel. God acknowledged this fact as such. His anger burned against them because they did not speak the truth about God as Job did (42:7). We don't know how teachable they were.

C. Consider the Pharisees and all of Israel at the time of Christ — how was Job's and the three friend's theology similar to the Pharisees? Answer: Doing is better than believing and trusting. Doing is the tool and the circumstances of life tell you and the world how good or bad you are. Believing that doing earns or keeps a person in God's smile is the key to the good life.

D. Job failed as a type of Christ: how? Answer: Job failed to see the big picture and got bogged down in his own circumstances. Jesus practiced long obedience in the same direction. Job demanded an explanation from God. God never gave him the answer he was looking for. Job came to know that God gave to him the best answer possible: Him!

VI. From your study of the book of Job, what have you learned about God, yourself, and your situation? Please be specific.

    A. How have you responded in and to your situation?

    B. How are you responding now?

    C. How has your view of God, yourself, and your situation changed?

    D. How are you responding differently than you have in the past?

Also by Dr. Jim Halla and Ambassador International

Being Christian in Your Medical Practice

Depression Through A Biblical Lens: A Whole-Person Approach

Endurance: What It Is and How It Looks in a Believer's Life

How to Be a God-Pleasing Patient: A Biblical Approach to Receiving Medical Care

Joy in Grief: God's Answer for Hard Times

Pain: The Plight of Fallen Man

Out of the Maze: A Covenant View of Hope

For more information about
Dr. Jim Halla
&

The Book of Job
please visit:

www.jimhalla.com
www.facebook.com/jimhalla
jimhalla@yahoo.com

For more information about
AMBASSADOR INTERNATIONAL
please visit:

www.ambassador-international.com
@AmbassadorIntl
www.facebook.com/AmbassadorIntl

Made in the USA
Middletown, DE
25 April 2022